telling itself. You learn about the multiplicity of cultures, their openness and permeability; that the boundaries between religions are not as hard and fast as we've been led to believe."
AAMER HUSSEIN, author of *37 Bridges*

"Amin Maalouf, one of the Arab world's most influential writers, weaves extraordinary tales in his novels, mixing historical events, romantic love, fantasy, and imagination. Yet at the core of all these well-crafted works lies a deep element of philosophical and psychological inquiry into the nature and condition of contemporary man."
AUB (American University of Beirut)

Praise for Adrift

"Across an impressive body of work, Maalouf has mapped out the points of rupture and convergence between Europe and the Arab World. In *Adrift*, using his own intellectual and political autobiography, he traces several of the turning points that have helped shape both his personal life and our world today. The lucid elegance of his analysis of complex and often chaotic events, is the paradox of this book and is among the many gifts of its gentle, learned and inquisitive author."
HISHAM MATAR

"Magnificent, a book of sorrows for our times, a provocative and powerful elegy by one of the world's great writers."
PHILIPPE SANDS

"With *Adrift*, Amin Maalouf again displays his supreme mastery in presenting the complexities of identity, history,

and politics. A great observer of the human condition, and himself a product of multiple cultures, Maalouf offers a penetrating and personal account of the troubled state of our planet and its peoples. No book is more evocative at capturing the richness of our cultures but also their fragility and the dangers that menace us all today."
BERNARD HAYKEL, Professor of Near Eastern Studies, Princeton University

"*Adrift* is both an elegy for the Levant in which he grew up, and a reflection on the violent fragmentation and political malaise of globalized capitalism. In Maalouf's portrait, the world in which COVID-19 made its calamitous appearance is disoriented and dangerously unequal, fragmented into identity-based groups, at war with one another yet all beholden to the market."
The London Review of Books

"The writer and scholar delves back into his own history to analyze the tragic consequences of the shock prophesized by Samuel Huntington."
Le Figaro Magazine

"True change is possible: Maalouf shows us possible ways forward in magnificent prose filled with wisdom."
La Provence

"Over rupture and conflict, Amin Maalouf has always preferred epics of encounters, beginnings, and connections."
Le Point

"A powerful voice."
France Culture

"An alarming report on the state of the world."
Le Soir

Praise for The Disoriented

"A thoughtful, philosophically rich story that probes a still-open wound."
Kirkus Reviews

"A powerful and nostalgic current of lost paradise and stolen youth."
Huffington Post

"A great, sensitive testimony on the vulnerability of the individual in an age of global migration."
STEFAN HERTMANS, author of *War and Turpentine* and *The Convert*

"There are novels which reverberate long after you've finished reading them. Amin Maalouf's *The Disoriented* is such a novel. This is a voyage between the Orient and the West, the past and the present, as only the 1993 Goncourt Prize winner knows how to write it."
Le Figaro

"Amin Maalouf gives us a perfect look at the thoughts and feelings that can lead to emigration. One can only be impressed by the magnitude and the precision of his introspection."
Le Monde des Livres

"Maalouf's new book, *The Disoriented*, marks his return to the novel with fanfare. It is a very endearing book."
Lire

"Maalouf makes a rare incursion into the twentieth century, and he evokes his native Lebanon in a state of war, a painful subject which until now he had only touched upon."
Jeune Afrique

"The great virtue of this beautiful novel is that it concedes a human element to war, that it unravels the Lebanese carpet to undo its knots and loosen its strings."
L'Express

"Amin Maalouf has an intact love of Lebanon inside him, as well as ever-enduring suffering and great nostalgia for his youth, of which he has perhaps never spoken of as well as he has in this novel."
Page des Libraires

"Full of human warmth and told in an Oriental style, this is a sensitive reflection told through touching portraits."
Notes Bibliographiques

"A great work, which explores the wounds of exile and the compromises of those who stay."
L'Amour des Livres

"What Maalouf discusses in this novel is nothing less than the conflict between the Arab world and the West.
A personal, honest search for the greatest challenge of current world politics."
De Volkskrant

"Maalouf manages to draw the reader into a beautiful story that honours friendship and loyalty as essential parts of a decent human existence. He does not judge his characters. No one is completely bad, no one is completely good, all of

his characters are recognizable people who are attractive because of their flaws."
De Wereld Morgen

"Maalouf addresses themes such as multiculturalism, friendship, and disruptive conflict in a pleasant style. *The Disoriented* is a book that enriches readers by providing insight into the memories and facts of life of people from other cultures."
Literair Nederland

"*The Disoriented* is the new, long-awaited novel by Amin Maalouf, and perhaps his most personal, emotional, and compelling. A novel about memory, friendship, love."
La Compagnia del Mar Rosso

Praise for Disordered World

"With his consciously nurtured multiple identity, Maalouf is just the sort of interlocutor this period needs. He reaches deep into unmined seams of cultural history, scything elegantly through cliché and conventional models of received wisdom."
Financial Times

"Should be prescribed reading in the Foreign Office and on the foreign desk of newspapers and the BBC."
The Spectator, Books of the Year

"Stimulating and provocative."
Sunday Times

"Maalouf is perfectly placed and wonderfully qualified to shed light on the pervasive sense that there is a cataclysmic battle in progress between civilisations and systems of belief. *Disordered World* is full of insight."
The Observer

Praise for Leo Africanus

"*Leo Africanus* is a beautiful book of tales about people who are forced to accept choices made for them by someone else—it relates, poetically at times and often imaginatively, the story of those who did not make it to the New World."
New York Times

"Utterly fascinating."
BBC World Service

"A celebration of the romance and power of the Arab world, its ideals and achievements."
Daily Telegraph

"Maalouf offers a lurid history lesson in this sweeping, sympathetic portrayal of Islamic culture of the period."
Publishers Weekly

Praise for The Garden of Light

"A fine, meditative historical novel from the internationally acclaimed Lebanese author."
Kirkus Reviews

"Maalouf's Mani has the ring of life—a sad, glowing book."
Washington Post

"Has the feel of a 1950s Hollywood epic, in which men gesture boldly and deliver words that deserve to be immediately carved in stone."
New York Times Book Review

Praise for In the Name of Identity

"Speaks from the depth of a powerful intellect."
The Times (London)

"His observation of human nature in all its facets is wonderfully accurate."
Sunday Telegraph

"This book sets out quite simply what is required of civilization in the third millennium."
Le Monde

"The clear, calm, cogent and persuasive voice from the Arab world that it seemed everyone in the West had been waiting for."
New York Times

"This is an important addition to contemporary literature on diversity, nationalism, race and international politics."
Publishers Weekly

Praise for The Crusades Through Arab Eyes

"Amin Maalouf has brilliantly reconstituted a semi-documentary narrative from 'the other side.'"
New York Times

"*The Crusades Through Arab Eyes* may be warmly recommended to lay-readers and students alike."
The Times Literary Supplement (London)

"A useful and important analysis adding much to existing Western histories."
London Review of Books

"A wide readership should enjoy this vivid narrative of stirring events."
The Bookseller

Praise for Balthasar's Odyssey

"Sparkling and erudite, this is a wonderful novel."
The Independent

"How Amin Maalouf in the distant past also shows the crises and opportunities of the present is masterly."
Die Zeit

"Both a meditation on the need for Christians, Muslims, and Jews to tolerate each other and a fantastic travelogue."
MICHÈLE ROBERTS, author of *Daughters of the House*

Praise for Samarkand

"Maalouf has written an extraordinary book, describing the lives and times of people who have never appeared in fiction before and are unlikely to do so again. The book is far more than a simple historical novel; like the intricate embroidery of an oriental carpet it weaves back and forth

through the centuries, linking the poetry, philosophy and passion of the Sufi past with modernism."
The Independent

"Maalouf creates a colorful custom painting of the then-Orient in front of the reader's inner eye and pulls out all the stops that a juicy historical novel should."
IRIS HETSCHER, *Weser Kurir*

Praise for Origins: A Memoir

"Maalouf holds to his elliptical narrative with spirit and finesse. The result is both exquisitely tempered and rudely compelling."
The Independent

"Maalouf has a novelist's ear for language and an historian's eye for detail: they have combined to create a masterpiece."
Tablet

"A terrific evocation of the mindset of a genuinely interesting family, and the times and nations through which they travelled."
The Fiction Desk

Praise for The Rock of Tanios

"Told with the simplicity of fable but set on the cusp of the modern world, this is a wonderful tale."
The Independent

"This is a beautifully crafted story detailing the intricacies of the folklores and superstitions which dominated nineteenth-century Oriental village life."
The Observer

Adrift

HOW OUR WORLD LOST ITS WAY

Amin Maalouf

Adrift

HOW OUR WORLD LOST ITS WAY

Translated from the French
by Frank Wynne

WORLD EDITIONS
New York, London, Amsterdam

Published in the USA in 2020 by World Editions LLC, New York
Published in the UK in 2020 by World Editions Ltd., London

World Editions
New York | London | Amsterdam

Printed by Lake Book, USA

Library of Congress Cataloging in Publication Data is available

ISBN 978-1-64286-075-7

First published as *Le naufrage des civilisations* in France in 2019 by Editions
Grasset & Fasquelle, Paris

Twitter: @WorldEdBooks
Facebook: @WorldEditionsInternationalPublishing
Instagram: @WorldEdBooks
www.worldeditions.org

Book Club Discussion Guides are available on our website.

For my mother, for my father
and for the fragile dreams
they bequeathed me

Prologue

The gods know the things of the future,
the full and sole possessors of all lights.
Of the future things, wise men perceive
approaching things. Their hearing

is sometimes, during serious studies,
disturbed. The mystical clamor
of approaching events reaches them.
And they heed it with reverence.

Constantine Cavafy (1863–1933)
The Complete Poems of Cavafy
(translated by Rae Dalven)

I was born hale and healthy into the arms of a dying civilization, and I have spent my whole life feeling that I am surviving, with no credit or blame, when around me so many things were falling into ruin; like those characters in films who walk down streets where all the walls are crumbling and yet emerge unscathed, shaking the dust from their clothes, while behind them the entire city is no more than a pile of rubble.

From my first breath, this has been my sad privilege. But it is also, doubtless, characteristic of our era when compared to those that came before. Time was, men had the impression of their being transient in a world that was immutable; people lived on the land where their parents had lived, worked as they did, cared for each other as they did, were educated as they had been, prayed in the same fashion and travelled by the same means. My four grandparents and their forebears for twelve generations were all born in the Ottoman dynasty, how could they not believe it would be eternal?

"Within the memory of a rose, no gardener had died," sighed the French philosophers of the Enlightenment, thinking about the social order and the monarchy of their own country. These days, the thinking roses that we are live longer, and gardeners die. In the span of a life, it is possible to see countries, empires, peoples, languages, and civilizations disappear.

Humanity is metamorphosing before our eyes. Never has its adventure seemed more promising, or more perilous. To a historian, the spectacle that is the world is fascinating. Yet he must still come to terms with his loved ones' anguish and his own fears.

I was born in a universe called the Levant, but it is so forgotten now that most of my contemporaries do not know to what I am referring.

True, no nation has ever borne this name. When books speak of the Levant, its history is vague, its geography shifting—little more than an archipelago of trading cities, often though not always coastal, running from Alexandria to Beirut, Tripoli, Aleppo, or Smyrna, from Baghdad to Mosul, Constantinople, Thessaloniki, from Odessa to Sarajevo.

In the outmoded sense in which I use it, it describes the territory wherein the ancient civilizations of the Middle East rubbed shoulders with the younger cultures of the West. From this intimacy was almost born a different future for all people.

I shall later discuss this wasted opportunity at greater length, but I need to say a word about it now in order to clarify my thoughts: if the citizens of different nations and the followers of the monotheistic religions had continued to live together in this part of the world and had managed to pool their fates, humanity as a whole would have had an eloquent beacon of peaceful coexistence and prosperity to inspire and to light the way. Regrettably, what happened was the reverse, hatred prevailed, and an inability to live together became the rule.

The Enlightenment of the Levant guttered out. Then shadows spread across the globe. And, to my mind, this is not simply a coincidence.

The Levantine ideal, as my people experienced it, as I have always wanted to live it, demands that each person assume full responsibility for himself, and a little responsibility for others. Like all ideals, it is something which we can aspire to though never quite attain. Though the aspiration is in itself salutary, it indicates the path we should follow: the path of reason, the path that leads to the future. In fact I would go so far as to say that, for a humane society, it is this aspiration that marks the passage from barbarism to civilization.

Throughout my childhood, I witnessed the joy and pride of my parents when they mentioned friends of different faiths or different countries. It was no more than a barely perceptible inflection in their voices. But it conveyed a message. A "user's manual," I would call it now.

At the time, it seemed to me so much a commonplace that I scarcely thought about it; I was convinced that this was how things were everywhere. Only much later did I realize that the closeness between the two communities in the world of my childhood was extremely rare. And extremely fragile. Early in life, I would see it tarnish, degrade, and disappear, leaving behind only nostalgia and shadows.

Was I right when I said that shadows spread over the globe when the Enlightenment of the Levant guttered out? Is it not incongruous for me to speak of shadows when I and my contemporaries have witnessed the most spectacular technological advances of all time; when we have at our fingertips the sum of human knowledge; when our fellow men live to a greater age and in better health than they did in the past; when so many former "Third World" countries, China and India first and foremost, have finally emerged from underdevelopment?

But this is precisely the tragic paradox of our century: for the first time in history we have the means to rid humanity of the scourges that have plagued it, to lead it towards an era of freedom, of unblemished progress, of global solidarity and shared wealth; and yet here we are, hurtling full-tilt in the opposite direction.

*

I am not one of those who likes to believe "things were better in my day." I am fascinated by scientific discoveries, enchanted by the liberation of bodies and minds, and I consider it a privilege to live in an era as inventive and as unrestrained as ours. However, despite this fascination, in recent years certain increasingly disturbing currents have threatened to destroy everything that our species has created, all the things of which we are justly proud, those things that we are accustomed to calling "civilization."

How have we come to this? This is the question I ask myself every time I am faced with the baleful upheavals of the century. How did we find ourselves adrift? What were the paths we should not have taken? Could we have avoided them? And is it still possible today to get things back on an even keel?

If I resort to naval terminology, it is because the image that has haunted me in recent years is that of a shipwreck—a gleaming modern ocean liner, as buoyant and reputedly unsinkable as the *Titanic*, carrying a crowd of passengers from every class and every country, sailing proudly towards its own destruction.

Does it need to be said that I am not simply an observer watching it pass? I am aboard, with all my contemporaries. With those I love most, with those I like least. With everything I have built, or believe that I have built. There is little doubt that, in the course of this book, I will attempt to maintain a level-headed tone. But I am terrified as I gaze at the mountainous mass of ice ahead. And I am fervent as I pray to heaven, after my fashion, that we can avoid it.

The shipwreck, it goes without saying, is metaphorical.

Necessarily subjective, necessarily approximate. It would be possible to come up with other images to describe the convulsion of the century. All those places whose names I love to say aloud—Assyria, Nineveh, Babylonia, Mesopotamia, Emesa, Palmyra, Tripolitania, Cyrenaica, or the Sabaean Kingdom, formerly known as Arabia Felix—their citizens, heirs to the most ancient civilizations, now flee on rafts as in the wake of the shipwreck.

In some cases, global warming is to blame. Vast glaciers that are melting; the Arctic Ocean, which, for the first time in millennia, is navigable in summer; great icebergs calved by Antarctica; the island nations of the Pacific worrying that soon they will be engulfed ... In the decades to come, will they experience an apocalyptic foundering?

In other cases, the image is more symbolic, it is less concrete, less poignant in its human cost. For example, when we consider Washington, the capital of the greatest global power, a state we would expect to set the example for adult democracy and exert a quasi-paternal authority over the rest of the world, does it not conjure the image of a shipwreck? There is no rickety vessel floating on the Potomac; but in a sense, it is the bridge deck of humanity that is flooded, and its passengers cast adrift.

In still other cases, what is at stake is Europe itself. Its dream of union is, to my mind, one of the most promising of our times. What has become of it? How have we allowed it to become so debased? When Great Britain decided to leave the European Union, officials from every country rushed to minimize the damage and promised bold initiatives to relaunch the project, and I hope with all my heart that they will succeed. In the meantime, I cannot help but murmur once again: "What a disaster!"

There is a long list of things that, only yesterday, could

make men dream, could lift their spirits, renew their energy, but that, today, have lost all lustre. I do not think it is an exaggeration to equate the "demonetization" of ideals, which continues to spread, and which is affecting every system, every doctrine, with a general moral shipwreck. While the communist utopia is sinking into the abyss, the triumph of capitalism has brought with it an obscene explosion of inequality. While it might be argued that, economically, this is its raison d'être, in human and ethical terms, it is unquestionably a disaster.

Do these few examples convey my meaning? Not sufficiently, to my mind. Although they may explain how I came to choose my title, they do not satisfactorily communicate the crux of my argument. Namely: we are caught up in a machine that no one deliberately set in motion, but one towards which we are forcibly being dragged, one that threatens to destroy our civilizations.

In talking about the turmoil that has led the world to the brink of this disaster, I will frequently feel compelled to use *I*, *me*, and *we*. I would rather not have used the first person, especially in a book that concerns all human endeavour, but how could I do otherwise when, from earliest childhood, I was a witness to the upheavals of which I am about to speak; when "my" Levantine universe was the first to go under; when it was the suicidal anguish of "my" Arab nation that dragged the whole planet into this catastrophic chain of events?

I

A Paradise in Flames

After the torchlight red on sweaty faces
After the frosty silence in the gardens
After the agony in stony places
The shouting and the crying
Prison and palace and reverberation
Of thunder of spring over distant mountains
He who was living is now dead
We who were living are now dying
With a little patience

T.S. Eliot (1888–1965)
The Waste Land

1

I did not know the Levant in its heyday, I arrived too late, all that was left of the spectacle was a tattered backcloth, all that remained of the banquet were a few crumbs. But I always hoped that one day the party might start up again, I did not want to believe that fate had seen me born into a house already condemned to demolition.

My people have built many houses, from Anatolia to Mount Lebanon, to coastal cities and the valley of the Nile, only to abandon them, one after another. I feel a nostalgia for them, unsurprisingly, and also a little stoic resignation when confronted by the vanity of things. Never become attached to something you might miss when the day comes that you must leave!

It was in Beirut that I was born, on February 25, 1949. The news was announced the following day, as was once customary, via a paragraph in the newspaper where my father worked: *Mother and child are both doing well.*

The country and the region, on the other hand, were doing badly. Few realized it at the time, but the descent into hell had already begun.

Egypt, the adoptive country of my mother's family, was in turmoil. On February 12, two weeks before my birth, Hassan al-Banna, founder of the Muslim Brotherhood, had been assassinated. He had gone to meet with one of his political allies; as he left the building, a car drew up and a gunman fired. Although shot in the chest, he did not collapse and the wound did not seem serious. He even managed to take cover behind the vehicle and note the license plate. This was how it was discovered that the car driven by his killers belonged to the Director-General of the Police.

Al-Banna then went to hospital to be treated. His supporters assumed that he would be discharged the same day with nothing more than a bandage. They were preparing to carry him through the streets in triumph, but he bled out from an internal haemorrhage. Within hours, he was dead. He was only forty-two.

His assassination was a response to that of the Egyptian Prime Minister, Nokrashy Pasha, gunned down by a member of the Muslim Brotherhood a month and a half earlier, on December 28. The killer, a medical student, had dressed as a police officer to infiltrate an official building, get close to the statesman, and shoot him at point-blank range as he was getting into a lift. A murder that may itself have been prompted by the government's decision on December 8 to disband the Brotherhood.

The struggle between the Islamic organization and the Cairo authorities had already been going on for twenty years. On the eve of my birth, it grew much more acrimonious. In the decades that followed, there would be many bloody incidents, long periods of truce invariably followed by more violence. As I write these lines, it is still going on.

This conflict, which began in Egypt in the 1920s, would in time see repercussions for the whole world, from the Sahara to the Caucasus, from the mountains of Afghanistan to the Twin Towers in New York, which were attacked and destroyed on September 11, 2001, by a suicide commando led by an Egyptian militant.

But in 1949, the clashes between the authorities and the Brotherhood, brutal though they were, had not yet affected day-to-day life. As a result, my mother had no hesitation in taking me and my older sister to Cairo four months after I was born. It was much easier for her to care for us with the help of her parents and the servants they employed. In Lebanon, my father, who worked as a newspaper editor, did not have the means to offer her the same luxuries. When he had the time, it was he who accompanied her to see her family. He did so without demur—he venerated Egypt's past and admired its teeming present—its poets, its artists, its musicians, its theatre, its cinema, its newspapers, its publishers ... In fact, it was in Cairo, in 1940, that he published his first book, an anthology of Levantine writers in English. And it was also in Cairo, at the Greek Catholic church, that my parents were married in 1945.

In those days, the country of the Nile was a second homeland for my family, and for three years, my mother took me there for long stays—just after I was born, the following year, and the year after. During the cool season, obviously, since in summer the air was said to be "unbreathable."

Then this custom was brutally interrupted. In the last days of 1951, my grandfather, whose name was Amin, died suddenly of a heart attack. And perhaps it was a blessing for him to leave this world before he saw his life's work fall to pieces. Because, less than a month later, *his* Egypt, the country he loved so much, was already in flames.

*

He had arrived at the age of sixteen, in the wake of his eldest brother, and had quickly found a place for himself thanks to a singular talent: training horses. If an animal was skittish, the teenager would jump on its back, wrap his arms and legs around it and not let go. However much the horse ran, reared, or tried to throw him, the rider hung on tightly. The horse always tired before he did. She would slow, bow her head, then pad towards the water trough to slake her thirst. My future grandfather would pat the horse's flanks, stroke her neck, run his fingers through her mane. He had broken her.

He did not practise the profession for long. When he was a few years older and a few kilos heavier, he launched into a completely different career, one for which he had no qualifications and no specific training, but one that Egypt, a country in rapid development, desperately needed: building roads, canals, and bridges. With his brothers, he set up a public works company in Tanta, a town on the Nile Delta. It was here that he would meet his wife, Virginie, a Maronite like himself, who had been born in Adana in Asia Minor: her family had fled to Egypt to escape the bloody massacres of 1909, which had begun by targeting Armenians before extending to other Christian communities.

My future grandparents were married in Tanta at the end of the First World War. They had seven children. Their first child, a son, died very young; then, in 1921, a daughter—my mother. They named her Odette. My father always called her Aude.

When the family business began to thrive, my grand-father moved and settled in Heliopolis, the new city built on the outskirts of Cairo by Baron Empain, a wealthy Belgian industrialist. At the same time, my grandfather was having a house built on Mount Lebanon, where he would spend the summer, a white stone house—solid, elegant, well located, and comfortable without being ostentatious.

Many of those who left to work in Egypt at the same time as my grandfather now live in opulent palaces;

they were proprietors of banks, factories, cotton fields, international companies. Moreover, many were awarded titles—Pasha, Count, Prince. This was not the case for my grandfather. He earned a good living, but he never amassed a fortune. Even in the village, where there were no more than twenty houses, his was not the most lavish. His hard work and determination allowed him to prosper, to rise above the conditions in which he had been born, but without reaching to the top of the social ladder. Truth be told, his career path was similar to that of many of his compatriots who in the late nineteenth and early twentieth centuries chose to settle in the Nile Valley rather than emigrate to more distant lands.

Having been born at the end of this period, I first knew about it through the tales told by my parents and their friends. Later, I read a little on the subject: stories, detailed reports, and also novels that celebrated the glories of Alexandria and Heliopolis. Today, I am convinced that, in their time, my forebears had excellent reasons to choose Egypt. It offered industrious emigrants opportunities since unrivalled.

It is true that other countries—the United States, Brazil, Mexico, Cuba, or Australia—offered almost boundless opportunities. This, however, meant crossing oceans and permanently cutting oneself off from one's native land, whereas my grandfather, at the end of an arduous year working, could return to his village to be cosseted and to recharge his batteries.

Later, much later, there would be a wave of emigration to oil-producing countries, which were closer, geographically, and where it was possible to earn a decent living, or, for the more cunning, to make a fortune—but nothing more. These emigrants worked hard, dreamed in silence, got drunk on the sly, then let off steam in conspicuous consumption. In the Nile Valley life was different, there were many kinds of cuisine. Music, literature, and many of the arts saw a cultural explosion that welcomed the participation of emigrants as much as that of the local population.

For some time, the composers, singers, actors, novelists, and poets of Egypt were the stars of the Arab world and beyond. While Umm Kulthum was singing the *Rubaiyat* of Omar Khayyam, and the unforgettable Asmahan, a Syrian émigré, crooned "Layali El Unse Fi Vienna," Leila Mourad, née Assouline, daughter of a long line of Jewish musicians, thrilled concert halls with her song "Mon cœur est mon seule guide."

This movement radiated out from the Levant and from the Arabic language to other cultures. It is significant, for example, that "My Way," a song forever associated with Frank Sinatra, was originally composed by a French-Egyptian, Claude François, before its lyrics were rewritten in English by Paul Anka, a Canadian of Syrian-Lebanese origin. In fact, even France's music-hall tradition has long been home to stars born in Egypt, such as Dalida, Georges Moustaki, Guy Béart, and indeed Claude François himself.

This is just one of many domains. When my grandfather visited the Egyptian Ministry for Public Works to discuss contracts, there was a civil servant working on another floor named Constantine Cavafy, who, unbeknownst to anyone at the time, would one day be considered the greatest modern Greek poet—born April 29, 1863, in Alexandria, died April 29, 1933, in Alexandria, according to his biographers. There is nothing to suggest that the two men ever met, but I like to imagine that they both pored over the same irrigation plan.

It was also in Alexandria that the great Italian poet Giuseppe Ungaretti was born in 1888, and lived as a child. His mother owned a bakery there ...

*

My father, who unlike many of his compatriots was not motivated by money, knew Egypt primarily through its poets. He would often recite their poems to me, and by dint of repetition I still remember some of them. His idol was Ahmed Shawqi, nicknamed the "Prince of Poets," who was the figurehead of an Arabic cultural renaissance that, at the time, people believed was inevitable, imminent, and could only blossom in the Valley of the Nile.

When Shawqi visited Lebanon it was a major event that warranted headlines in the newspapers. Wherever he went, he was surrounded by a flock of young writers. To the end of his days, my father was proud that he had once met him. It happened in an open-air restaurant, where the poet had poured beer into a glass, brought it up to his ear, and, tilting his head back slightly, explained to the assembled company that Arabic writers of an earlier age had given a name to this characteristic sound: *jarsh.* It is a detail of no great importance, but my father was always emotional when he told this story, since it brought back to his mind the voice, the gesture of the great Shawqi.

When I find myself in Rome, I sometimes go to the park of the Villa Borghese, where there is a statue of the Egyptian poet seated, wearing a bow tie, holding a rose, head tilted back slightly just as in my father's memory.

Just as important as "Prince" Shawqi, and just as representative of an era filled with promise, was Taha Hussein, nicknamed the "Dean of Arabic Letters."

Taha Hussein was born into a poor family in a small village, and became blind at the age of three as the result of a poorly treated infection, but he managed to overcome his disadvantages to become the most highly respected Egyptian intellectual of modern times. A man of the Enlightenment, resolutely modernist, he encouraged Arabic researchers to reanalyse history with the aid of modern scientific tools rather than simply accepting the received ideas of their predecessors.

A turbulent dispute erupted in 1926, when he published a book in which he argued that a particular body of poetry considered pre-Islamic had actually been entirely rewritten at a later date as part of a rivalry between different tribes. This was considered scandalous, and Hussein was branded an infidel; he called into question not only the accepted canon of Arabic literature, but the manner in which the works had been written. Scholars were determined to prevent him from applying his iconoclastic methods to religious texts.

The dispute called to mind another, one triggered sixty-four years early by Ernest Renan when, during his inaugural lecture at the Collège de France, he dared to refer to Jesus as an "exceptional man," without considering him to be God. Taha Hussein was suspended from his post as professor at the University of Cairo, just as Renan had been. But when the Grand Imam of al-Azhar, the highest religious authority in the country, demanded that he be put on trial, the Egyptian government refused to take this drastic step, considering that the judicial system had no role in academic debate.

Despite the attacks he suffered from traditional scholars, the Dean of Arabic Letters remained an eminent intellectual to his dying day, an academic who was respected by his contemporaries and one who was appointed to a number of eminent positions: Head of the Department of Literature, Rector of the University of Alexandria, and, from 1950–52, Minister for National Education—or, to employ the splendid term used in Egypt at the time, "Minister of Knowledge." One of his first decisions was to call for free education.

That a blind man, seen by certain authorities as a heretic, could have had such a meteoric career obviously speaks volumes about Taha Hussein, but it also says much about the Egypt of his time.

I could give dozens of similar examples. I could mention that it was the Cairo Opera House, in 1871, that saw the first performance of Verdi's *Aida*, a commission by the Khedive of Egypt; I could conjure the names Youssef Chahine or Omar Sharif, both Egyptians of Lebanese descent, who rose from the Egyptian film industry to triumph on the world stage; I could cite numerous specialists who agree that the School of Medicine in Cairo was, for a time, one of the finest in the world … But I am not trying to prove something, I am simply trying to convey the impression I got from my parents: that of an exceptional country experiencing a privileged moment in its history.

I have evoked memories of my father, but it was chiefly my mother who spoke to me endlessly about Egypt, every day of her life. About its mangos and guavas "whose flavour can be found nowhere else in the world"; about Cicurel, the Cairo department store "that was easily the equal of Harrods in London or the Galeries Lafayette in Paris"; about Groppi, a patisserie "as good as any in Milan or Vienna"; not to mention the long, languorous beaches of Alexandria …

Of course, a part of this was the commonplace nostalgia anyone in the twilight years of life might feel when recalling their gilded youth. But there was more to it than that; my mother's word was not my only evidence. I have listened to so many people, read so many accounts that there is no doubt in my mind that—for one shining moment, for a particular section of the population—there was a paradise called Egypt. A place I visited before I could see it, before I could understand, before I could form memories. And which, one day, ceased to be what once it was, and ceased to promise what once it had.

2

When my grandfather was buried in the Maronite cemetery in Cairo, in the early days of January 1952, the streets were as peaceful as always, although the tension was palpable to those who could sense it.

For three months, a crisis had been brewing between the national government and the British authorities, who had granted the country independence thirty years earlier, only to later, in 1936, compel it to sign a treaty that allowed British troops to be stationed in the zone around the Suez Canal. At that time, Mussolini's invasion of Ethiopia and the rise of Hitler justified such an arrangement. But since the end of the Second World War, the Egyptian authorities had been asking London to put an end to a military presence that served no purpose, was incompatible with the sovereignty of the country, and was resented by its citizens.

Negotiations began, proposals and counter-proposals were exchanged, interminable talks led to no concrete result. Exasperated, in October 1951, the government in Cairo voted to unilaterally abrogate the treaty and demanded that the British withdraw their presence immediately. This stance was greeted enthusiastically by Egyptians, who spontaneously took to the streets to celebrate the "liberation" of the territory, as though it were a fait accompli.

But London had no intention of complying. A new prime minister was in power, none other than Winston Churchill. Having suffered a humiliating defeat in 1945, following a military victory of which he had been the chief architect, he had just won a general election at the age of seventy, and retaken the reins of power. This was a man who had lost nothing of his obstinacy. He resented the Labour Party for giving up the Indian colonies and was determined not to concede another square inch of empire, nor an ounce of prestige. Rather than withdraw his troops from the Suez Canal zone, he dispatched reinforcements.

His Egyptian counterpart, Mostafa el-Nahas Pasha, was also an experienced politician. At the age of seventy-two, he was leading the fifth government of his long career. A rich landowner, temperate in his patriotism and in favour of Western-style parliamentary democracy, he did not particularly relish the idea of crossing swords with Great Britain. But he could not back down without losing face, or being outflanked by more militant nationalists.

He resorted to several strategies intended to tire the British so they would agree to leave of their own accord. It was a risky policy, very risky—as we shall see—but he felt that to appear to collaborate with the occupying forces was yet a greater risk.

To some, the measures adopted by the Egyptian authorities were purely symbolic. In Alexandria, various streets were renamed, stripping them of the names of British generals like Lord Kitchener and General Allenby. In Cairo, it was decided to transform Gezira Sporting Club, the exclusive private club frequented by British expatriates, into a public garden open to all. Merchants were encouraged not to import British products. The tens of thousands of Egyptians who worked for the British Armed Forces in the Canal Zone were urged to quit their jobs, with promises of compensation and threats of reprisals if they continued in the service of the occupying forces.

More seriously, commando attacks were carried out on

the British garrison by armed men who came from various political movements, from communist, to nationalist, to the Muslim Brotherhood. Some of these militants were members of the police forces and so, to prevent matters slipping beyond their control, the government gave permission for police auxiliaries to take part in the attacks.

The British decided to strike back hard, to set an example. On Friday, January 25, 1952, they launched an assault on the police headquarters in Ismailia, on the western bank of the canal. There ensued a pitched battle that resulted in the death of forty Egyptians and left hundreds wounded. When news spread through the country, it provoked the wrath of the whole nation.

By dawn the following day, protesters had already begun to gather in the streets of Cairo. As the hours passed, their numbers swelled, and they began to loot and burn the most obvious British businesses—Barclays Bank, Thomas Cook, W.H. Smith, the Turf Club, and Shepheard's Hotel, built a century earlier, which had once served as headquarters to the British Army and was among the most opulent hotels in the country.

As the day wore on, the rioters extended their attacks to any business frequented by Westerners or by the Egyptian ruling classes: bars, private clubs, cinemas, and Western-style department stores—among them the unforgettable Cicurel that my mother so loved. Everywhere was looted, pillaged, and razed to the ground; there were even a number of lynchings. By the end of the day, there were thirty people dead, some five hundred injured, and more than a thousand buildings had been burned. The modern centre of the capital was completely devastated.

Those responsible for the great Cairo fire were never identified. Even today, some historians believe it was a spontaneous protest that got out of hand, feeding on its own destructive rage, while others are convinced it was directed by an unseen hand with specific political goals. The fact remains that, as the hours passed, the slogans grew louder. Although at first the demonstrators were only protesting against the actions of the British soldiers, later on the crowd began to chant slogans that were hostile to the Egyptian government, whom they accused of complicity, and even the young King Farouk, who was said to be corrupt, indifferent to the sufferings of his subjects, and completely under the influence of his debauched friends.

Overwhelmed and powerless, the authorities did nothing to quell the riots, but simply protected the residential areas where high-ranking members of the regime lived. Utterly discredited, Nahas Pasha was forced to resign the following morning. He had lost his wager and would never again play a significant role in his country. And he was not the only one. The former ruling class would soon be forced out, never to return.

*

Six months after the Cairo fire, the "Free Officers Movement" seized power, the king went into exile, and a new era began, one characterized by a bitter struggle between two major political forces, both fiercely nationalist and bitterly opposed to the cosmopolitan society that had formerly existed: on the one hand, the Muslim Brotherhood, which enjoyed huge popular support; on the other, the armed forces, from whose ranks a strongman emerged, Colonel Gamal Abdel Nasser. For the next fifteen years he would be the most popular leader in the Arab world, and one of the most visible players on the world stage.

For my family, however, his rise to power was an ominous sign. The new strongman repeatedly insisted that the Egyptian people should wrest control of its territory, its resources, and its destiny from the hands of foreigners. In the years that followed the 1952 Revolution, a panoply of measures was passed—seizures, confiscations, sequestrations, expropriations, nationalizations, etc.— intended to strip landowners of their assets, with particular attention, I might add, to those who had the misfortune to be non-native.

My grandfather died before the Cairo fire and the Revolution, but his heirs would soon be forced to sell off the properties he had bequeathed them for a fraction of their value. And later forced to leave their native Egypt, in confusion; some for North America, the others for Lebanon.

While my family was grieving for its lost paradise, Nasser was growing in stature and consolidating his power. In a series of skilful manoeuvres, he succeeded in sidelining his rivals in the military and emerged victorious in the trial of strength that pitted him against the Muslim Brotherhood. Now President of the Republic and undisputed leader of the revolution, he decided that the time had come to give Egyptians their revenge on the British. On July 26, 1956, during a speech in Alexandria, he announced the nationalization of the Universal Company of the Maritime Canal of Suez, and that same day Egyptian forces seized control of the canal. Some weeks later, Great Britain, France, and Israel launched a concerted military attack—but this had to be abandoned.

Denounced by Washington and threatened with reprisals from Moscow, the three countries were forced to cease their operations and withdraw their troops.

The Suez Crisis proved to be a major political debacle for the two principal colonial powers, and was a triumph for Nasser. He had given his people a dazzling revenge; he had succeeded in silencing his Islamist critics for years to come; and he had stepped onto the world stage as the new champion of the oppressed.

It was at this point that the *Rais* signed the death warrant of liberal, cosmopolitan Egypt. He instigated a series of measures intended to hound the British, the French, and the Jews out of the country. In theory, these were "targeted" sanctions against those who had taken part in the "Tripartite Aggression." In practice, the policy triggered a mass exodus of what were called "Egyptianized" communities, many of whom had lived on the banks of the Nile for generations, or indeed centuries.

The measure solicited outrage only among those who were directly targeted. In the eyes of the rest of the world, given the context at the time, it seemed like a natural and predictable sequel to the Suez Crisis and to Egypt finally taking back the sovereignty it had so long been denied.

Overnight, Nasser became an idol to the masses, in his own country, in the Middle East, and beyond. No Arab leader in centuries had given rise to greater hopes than this handsome thirty-year-old officer with his intoxicating voice and his powerful speeches. But in my family, when his name was mentioned it was rarely to praise him, to bless him, or to wish him a long life.

3

My mother's family always felt that they had been unjustly banished from an earthly paradise.

Banished, they had certainly been, or at the very least forcibly manhandled towards the gates ... As to whether this was *unjust*, the matter deserves some consideration. My feeling on the subject has changed more than once over the years.

In my childhood, as one might expect, I shared the same convictions as my family. I listened to my mother's tales about what "we" had lost in Heliopolis or Alexandria, and they saddened me. It was a recurring theme at family gatherings. From time to time, some uncle or cousin or friend of the family would arrive in Lebanon having tried to stay in Egypt before throwing in the towel. I still remember the phrase used by one of those "demi-migrants" to describe life under the new revolutionary regime, which had drastically limited freedom of expression and freedom of association together with free enterprise: "These days, everything that's not forbidden is compulsory!" I have never forgotten that phrase, which seems to me an excellent definition of authoritarianism.

There were sordid episodes, too. As when a sinister character came to visit my mother and my uncles and offered to retrieve valuable objects from their house in Heliopolis whose export was prohibited by the Egyptian authorities. He claimed to have contacts in the customs department. Having little choice, my family decided to believe him. But of all the things entrusted to him, they saw nothing, or almost nothing. He had clearly taken them for himself and sold them. Needless to say, there could be no question of filing a complaint ...

Later, when I began to follow world events more closely, I began to see things in a different light. This was an era of national liberation, of the right of peoples to self-determination, of the struggle against colonialism and imperialism, against the looting of the Third World, against foreign military bases. If I had persisted in seeing the Egyptian Rais merely as the scourge he had been to my family, I would have felt as though I were placing our narrow interests above universal principles.

And so I found myself admiring our "despoiler," and listening to his speeches with a certain empathy. From time to time, I would defend him if I felt he was being unfairly attacked. I was encouraged in this by a friend of the family, a Lebanese-Egyptian man who often came to lunch with us. Although he had suffered, as had my family, from the measures adopted by the revolution, he had a boundless admiration for Nasser, and he made no bones about saying so whatever the circumstances. This triggered long, heated discussion, but rarely lasting disagreements. Everyone remained civilized and polite. If the Rais suffered a setback, my parents would tease their friend, and he in turn would taunt them when his hero scored some victory.

My feelings about the great man were very conflicted. They still are to this day. Even now, after all the years that have passed, I am undecided about him. From a certain viewpoint, Nasser was the last colossus of the Arab world, perhaps its last chance to get back on its feet. However, he was so sadly mistaken about so many fundamental issues that, in his wake, he left only bitterness, regret, and disillusionment. He abolished pluralism in favour of a one-party system; he muzzled the press that, under the old regime, had enjoyed considerable freedom; he relied on the secret services to silence his opponents;

his management of the Egyptian economy was bureau-cratic, inefficient, and ultimately ruinous; his national-istic demagoguery led him to the brink of the abyss, and the whole Arab world along with him ...

As you can see, I have significant reservations about his career without having to introduce the "self-centred" element, by which I mean the fact that he expelled my family from paradise.

*

I sometimes think that in a museum of universal history there should be a gallery called the "Pantheon of Janus." Here, under the aegis of the god with two faces, would be people of great stature who have played a historic role worthy of admiration, while also, and sometimes simul-taneously, playing a hateful, even destructive role. Two of the great men I have mentioned deserve places of hon-our in this Pantheon: Nasser and Churchill.

In the case of Nasser, later in this book I will discuss some of the policies that make him sympathetic and which explain why his untimely death evokes a certain nostalgia in me, and in many Arabs, while at the same time he was undeniably one of the gravediggers who interred the Levant I so loved. Without wishing to linger too much on this ambivalence, I will say that Nasser, like so many of his generation, grew up with a fierce resent-ment of foreign domination, and he marshalled all his energy to bring this to an end, without realizing that, in demolishing it, he was also destroying the way of life that came with it, and that, with a few minor adjust-ments, might have constituted a crucial factor in prog-ress and modernization.

In the case of Churchill, I need hardly say that his dogged fight against Nazism was a force for good. Without his energy, his determination, and his skill, Great Britain might have given up the fight, America might not have joined the war, and a great darkness would have settled over the world. To paraphrase one of his own speeches: "never was so much owed by so many" ... to one man.

Nevertheless, when we study his actions in the Arab world, we see a very different face. His legendary obstinacy, so admirable in the face of Hitler, was less than admirable when dealing with the great Nahas Pasha—a moderate patriot, a westernized patrician, a courageous modernist who went so far as to entrust the Ministry of Education to a renaissance figure like Taha Hussein.

It goes without saying that Churchill's goal was not to thwart the peaceful and harmonious development of Egypt. He simply wanted to protect the interests of the British Crown at all costs, heedless of the potential consequences of his actions. But the consequences were calamitous. If it hadn't been for the massacre of January 25, 1951—which if Churchill did not order, he authorized—a different form of patriotism might have prevailed, and the future of Egypt and of the Arab world might have taken a very different path.

The great man's responsibility is even clearer in the case of Iran. Churchill personally went to great lengths to bring down the government of Mohammad Mosaddegh, a democratic modernist whose sole crime was to ask that the Iranian people get a greater share of oil revenues. Today, we have the documents that prove that the British Prime Minister personally lobbied Washington to spearhead the 1953 Iranian coup d'état.

And so, Churchill's actions in Egypt fostered the emergence of an Arab nationalism that was authoritarian and xenophobic; meanwhile, his actions in Iran paved the way for Khomeini's brand of Islamism. In all good conscience, I presume, in both cases ...

*

But I will leave that digression to return to my original question: was my family unjustly banished from their paradise or did they deserve their fate?

If it is a matter of knowing how they felt during those years, I think I know them, and I will make no attempt to deny the obvious: like most Egyptianized people, whether Syrian, Lebanese, Italian, French, Greek, Jewish, or Maltese, they certainly preferred the reign of the pashas to that of the colonels. The status quo favoured them, they hoped it might continue indefinitely. And even if they had little sympathy for British Imperial policies, they saw the British as the guarantors of stability.

My mother told me that, during the great fire, fearing that the rioters would overrun Heliopolis and wreak the same havoc they had in the centre of Cairo, she had considered taking the car and driving with her mother to the Canal Zone, which was held by the British. She abandoned the idea only because the roads were not safe.

Hardly a patriotic standpoint, I willingly admit. But what should she have done? Meekly wait for a rampaging horde of arsonists? In the end, the arsonists stopped before they reached Heliopolis. "Our" house was saved. But only to be sold for a song some time later, when they were forced to leave the country forever.

Caught between the two uncontrollable forces of mounting Arabic fury and Western arrogance lashing out left and right with all the subtlety of a maddened elephant, my family were lost, no matter what they did. They were condemned not for their opinions, their statements, or their actions, but for their origins, which they had not chosen, and which they could not change.

Therefore, I will not attach much importance to their reactions during these turbulent years. The world had begun to founder, and so they clutched at any straw, clung to any piece of floating wreckage they hoped would save them from drowning—be it a king, a pasha, a foreign army. They may not have been innocent, but neither were they guilty.

4

With the passing of the years, and in light of what has happened in recent decades, the moral dilemma that has haunted me since adolescence now seems unwarranted. I have ceased to question whether my family, like the majority of Egyptianized people, deserved their fate, and whether Nasser had the right to brutally expel them from the country in which they were born.

Today, I am convinced that the appropriate response is the one adopted by another great African leader, one who was born in the same year as Nasser but appeared on the national stage somewhat later: Nelson Mandela. When, having spent twenty-six years imprisoned by the apartheid regime, he emerged triumphant and was elected President of South Africa, he did not ask himself whether white South Africans had supported him in the struggle for liberation; whether they had set aside their colonialist arrogance and their sense of superiority; whether they had integrated with the local populace in a spirit of respect and fraternity and whether, therefore, they deserved to be a part of this new nation ... The answer in every case would have been "No." Instead, Mandela wisely chose not to ask. He had a very different question in mind: will my country be better off if the Afrikaners stay rather than leave? And the answer seemed obvious to him: for the stability of South Africa, for the sake of its economy, the smooth running of its institutions, its image in the rest of the world, it was better to keep the white minority, regardless of how they had behaved before that point. And the new president did everything he could to persuade his former enemies not to desert the country.

One of the most symbolic moments was when, setting

aside the bitterness of the past and the euphoria of his victory, he went to visit Elizabeth Verwoerd, the widow of the Prime Minister who had had him imprisoned, to take tea and reassure her about the future.

Were his actions motivated by magnanimity or by political shrewdness? The truth is that it does not matter. We are wrong when we systematically pit personal interests against universal principles. Sometimes, the two converge. Sometimes, magnanimity is shrewd and pettiness is a mistake. Though our cynical world may be reluctant to admit it, history is filled with powerful examples. Often, when a country betrays its principles, it betrays its own interests.

The first case that comes to mind is that of Louis xiv when, in 1685, he revoked the Edict of Nantes, signed by his grandfather Henry iv to extend freedom of religion to the Protestant minority. Forced to flee France, those who were known as the Huguenots were welcomed in other European countries and handsomely contributed to the prosperity of Amsterdam, London, and Berlin; in the case of Berlin, many historians date its emergence as a metropolis to the arrival of the French refugees, a particularly eloquent detail since we know that in time it would become Paris's greatest rival.

The mass expulsion of the Huguenots impoverished France and enriched its rivals. The same might be said about the expulsion of the Muslims or the Jews by Catholic kings following the Granada War in 1492. It was this policy, dictated by intolerance and arrogance, which left Spain unable to exploit its conquest of the Americas; it would be five hundred years before it caught up with other European nations.

The only excuse to be found for the rulers who made

these disastrous decisions is that their short-sighted view was so commonplace at the time that it was mistaken for wisdom. Did they not have the right to believe that their kingdoms would be stronger for being more homogenous? And that Heaven would reward them, would shower them with graces, for having expelled the "heretics" and the "infidels"? In the real world, that is not how things go. Neither in the fifteenth century, the seventeenth, nor today. Throughout the course of history, mass expulsions—whether or not they seemed justified—have generally done more harm to those who stayed than to those who were forced to leave. There is no doubt that the exiles suffer to begin with, but, generally, they steel themselves, they overcome their trauma, and they often bring great wealth to the countries that have welcomed them.

It is no coincidence that the United States, the most powerful country in the world, has welcomed wave upon wave of the banished and exiled, from English Puritans to German Jews, by way of those fleeing revolutions in Russia, China, Cuba, or Iran, to say nothing of the French Protestants—the middle name of President Franklin Delano Roosevelt is a corruption of a Huguenot ancestor named De Lannoy.

*

I will return more than once to the perverse myth of homogeneity—religious, ethnic, linguistic, racial, or otherwise—that has deluded so many countries. For the moment, I would like to focus more specifically on the subject of people perceived as "foreign," and the function they can fulfil in the societies in which they live.

Often, minorities are pollinators. They fly, they flutter,

they gather pollen, and this can make them seem like profiteers, even parasites. It is only when they disappear that one becomes aware of the vital role they played.

The resentment felt by colonized peoples towards those who colonized them is understandable, and it is normal that they may harbour feelings of suspicion or even hostility towards those who supported and were protected by their former masters. Nevertheless, recent decades have taught us that the struggle for liberation is quickly followed by the struggle for development and modernization. In this second phase, the presence of an educated minority with direct access to industrialized societies is a crucial asset. One might compare it to an artery connecting the nascent country to the beating heart of the developed world. To cut this artery is absurd, it is self-mutilation, it is suicidal. It is something from which many countries never recover.

In the aftermath of a gruelling struggle, hostility and suspicion are understandable. But a great leader must be both a visionary and a pragmatist; he must be able to rise above visceral resentment, to persuade his comrades-in-arms, his countrymen that their priorities have changed, that, in the very moment of victory, their bitter enemies become valuable partners. Because of their connections to the economic and intellectual hub of the planet. And also, because their former privileged position means they have unrivalled expertise. Mandela was even able to win over the army and police—the very instruments of repression under the apartheid regime—and put them at the service of the "Rainbow Nation."

Nasser achieved none of these things, but I am not about to condemn him. He rose to power forty years before Mandela; and, even leaving aside the differing characters of the two men, there is no doubt that in the meantime the world had changed. In many ways, the Rais was a prisoner of the accepted ideas of his time. Colonialism was not yet a closed chapter in human history. After all, had not the downfall of Mosaddegh clearly demonstrated that the West, when driven out, could return in force to regain the upper hand?

In terms of the economy, which was to prove a crucial area, the Rais failed to see how the exceptional skills of the Egyptianized community could be useful to the country; in the 1950s and 1960s socialism and interventionism, the nationalization and state management of companies, still seemed to offer a promising economic future.

To these instances of "short-sightedness" one must add others, which cannot be easily explained away by the period or by the prevailing ideology of the time. In particular, I am thinking of a typical characteristic of Arab political life, one that in recent history has become a gaping wound. I would define it as the morbid inability to resist one-upmanship. Nasser constantly felt that he needed to prove he was more nationalistic than the Muslim Brotherhood and more radical than other nationalist leaders. Even after he rose to become the undisputed leader of Egypt and the hero of the Arab world, he was terrified that he might be outflanked by someone "more Nasser than he was."

And so, one day, fearing he might be accused of laxity, he allowed himself to be dragged into a war he did not want, one that would prove ruinous for him and for the country that had placed its faith in him.

I will return at length to the traumatic events of 1967, by which time my family had long since left Egypt. Needless to say, they still talked about it constantly, with that admixture of tenderness and bitterness.

As for me, I was eight years old when I visited our old house in Heliopolis for the last time. My mother took me to help pack up some things before we finally abandoned the place for good. My grandmother had just passed away from cancer. The house had been in her name, as was typical at the time, and she sold it on her deathbed to an Egyptian army officer. For a fraction of its value, needless to say, although she made the buyer promise to keep the statue of Saint Teresa that adorned the facade. She had brought this statue from Italy twenty-five years earlier so that it might watch over her new house.

The officer was true to his word, as were his heirs. As far as I know, Saint Teresa is still there.

5

My mother's paradise was irretrievably lost, and those turbulent times almost destroyed my father's paradise too. But Lebanon on this occasion managed to "dodge between the raindrops"; it was granted a stay of execution. In hindsight, one might say it was granted a last golden age.

By the time I opened my eyes to the world around me in the 1960s, Beirut had replaced Cairo as the intellectual capital of the Middle East. Even as Nasser was becoming the most influential political figure in the region, he was using the absolute power he wielded in Egypt to silence newspapers, publishers, academics, and political movements. And so the agora, the forum for debate in the Arab world, had moved to neutral territory, to a country where no repressive power held sway.

In this case, to Lebanon: no other country was better placed to play this role. Lebanon, being home to numerous communities of very different sensibilities, none of which could claim a hegemonic position, was a place where ideas and pluralism could thrive. All those who could no longer speak out in their own country naturally flocked here.

Neighbouring countries were becoming increasingly hostile to those who were not—or were no longer—in power. This was particularly true of Syria.

Few people now remember the era when Syria still had a free press, held free and fair elections contested by a wide range of political parties. Such a time once existed, though I do not remember it personally, since it was in March 1949, a month after I was born, that Damascus suffered its first military coup. The Chief of Staff of the Syrian Army, Husni al-Za'im, seized power and immediately suspended the Constitution. In June that same year, he was elected President with 99% of the vote, and named himself Marshal. In August, he was overthrown by a second military coup and summarily executed. Then, in December, a third coup resulted in his executioner being overthrown and assassinated a few months later ...

Since 1949, the year of the three military coups, democracy has never again managed to take root in Syria. In the decades since, the country has been beset by tragic and frustrating periods of instability alternating with dictatorships. And after each new upheaval, those who lost sought refuge in Lebanon—the dismissed army officers, the politicians who escaped from prisons, the industrialists whose factories had been nationalized, the artists and intellectuals seeking somewhere they could be free ...

For decades, a steady stream of refugees fled Damascus for Beirut. Those who had belonged to the Syrian elite easily integrated with the elite of their adoptive home. Nobody was offended to discover that such and such a Lebanese poet, actress, composer, government minister, or even president had in fact been born in Damascus, Aleppo, or Latakia rather than Beirut or Tyre.

I have dwelt on the case of Syria, by far the most striking, but the phenomenon is much older and more widespread. Lebanon has long been a safe haven for the "unloved" of the Middle East. Just as, after a fashion, Egypt had been until the 1940s. Seen in hindsight, this might give the false impression of a parallel between these two Levantine societies. In fact, they were built on very different foundations.

In Egypt, cosmopolitanism was linked to the long tradition of *échelles*, free-trade zones in the Muslim world where European citizens benefited from the protection of consuls appointed by the Allied Powers in accordance with inequitable treaties imposed on the Ottoman Empire, that erstwhile "sick man of Europe." Clearly the political environment had changed, but a number of practices continued. If an Italian living in Egypt murdered his neighbour, he could ask to be tried in Italy, and the local authorities had no right to object.

This is no random example; it is inspired by a true story that made the headlines in my grandparents' day. In March 1927, Solomon Cicurel, owner of the aforementioned emporium "Les Grands Magasins Cicurel," was murdered in his home in Cairo, having been stabbed eight times. The police had no trouble tracking down the killers: his driver, a former employee he had recently fired, and two accomplices. Of the four, two were Italian nationals and were handed over to the authorities of their home country without trial; a third, who was Greek, was deported to Greece; only the fourth, a man named Dario Jacoel, whose papers described him as a "stateless Jew," was tried and convicted. He, too, claimed to be Italian, and a member of the Fascist Party, but could supply no proof. Although it was clear he had played only a minor role, he was said to be the "driving force behind the crime," and duly hanged.

The case caused considerable outrage. Eminent Egyptian intellectuals took up the pen to denounce this ludicrous situation that meant foreign nationals were above the law, according them a form of diplomatic immunity, if not outright impunity.

Such excessive privileges aroused both envy and resentment. Some sectors of Egyptian society tried to forge close ties with Westerners so that they might enjoy the same benefits. But most people saw the status of foreign nationals as an affront to the country's independence and its dignity. The burning of Cairo was proof of this intense, simmering rage. Over the years, many similar incidents would take place in countries throughout the region, all triggered by similar resentments.

Some of these would have serious and lasting consequences. For example, the rift between Ayatollah Khomeini and the Shah of Iran occurred in 1964, when, having been pressured by the United States, the Shah agreed that US soldiers based in Iran could not be tried by local courts. So began an acrimonious dispute that, fifteen years later, would culminate in the overthrow of the monarchy and the founding of the Islamic Republic ... I have no doubt that there were many reasons behind the revolution—which I will return to later—but anger at the extraterritorial rights enjoyed by Westerners was unquestionably a factor. Nor is it a coincidence that one of the first acts of the Iranian revolutionaries was to flout the diplomatic immunity of the American Embassy and take hostages.

This, it goes without saying, was a flagrant violation of international norms. But it was primarily an act of rebellion against a "world order" that had prevailed for centuries, and which—explicitly or implicitly—established a pecking order among peoples and cultures, with the West enthroned at the top.

For the peoples forced to endure it, this discriminatory system had always been humiliating; and in the twilight years of colonialism, it had become unacceptable. Everything associated with colonialism was angrily and contemptuously dismissed. Even those few positive effects it could legitimately be said to have in its favour. Such as having fostered a certain kind of cultural "paradise" in Shanghai, in Calcutta, in Algiers or Alexandria, where delicate flowers grew from exceptional encounters between different languages and faiths, different wisdoms and traditions.

This sublime blossoming was doomed to be fleeting. Built as it was on such inequitable foundations, it could not possibly survive. As for those communities who were considered "foreign," even if they were not responsible for the circumstances that ensured their privileged status, they appeared guilty because they benefited from the system. And they ended up paying the price. This was what happened to the Syrian-Lebanese and the Greeks in Egypt, to the Italians in Libya, to the French *pieds noirs* in Algeria.

I wish the cultural world that produced Cavafy, Camus, Ungaretti, or Asmahan could have transformed and adapted instead of vanishing completely; but it must be accepted that the foundations on which it was built were rotten.

The Egypt of my mother's family was doomed to crumble. It was no more than a relic, the dying witness of a bygone age. Nasser administered the *coup de grâce*, and Egypt never recovered.

*

Lebanon was not in the same situation. Here, no category of citizen enjoyed extraterritorial rights. The aim of the country's founders was to foster a balance and a peaceful coexistence between local religious communities— Maronite, Druze, Sunni Muslim, Shia Muslim, Greek Orthodox, or Greek-Catholic, to say nothing of the Armenians, Syriacs, Jews, Alawites, and Ismailis.

Many of these communities had lived here since time immemorial, others had arrived only decades earlier, but none were considered "foreign"; when I was a child, it would have been considered inappropriate and downright rude to make distinctions between "natives" and "foreigners" or between those born in Lebanon and those who had recently arrived. Here was an example of Levantine society untainted by the original sin which corrupted cosmopolitan pluralism in Egypt.

Sadly, the system had its flaws. In particular, there was a tendency among the various Lebanese communities to appeal to other countries for protection in order to strengthen their position within their own. An equivalent would be Switzerland (to which Lebanon has often been compared); if the cantons of Zurich, Geneva, and Ticino appealed for protection to Germany, France, and Italy every time they had a disagreement, the Swiss Confederation would long since have disbanded.

"In the beginning, we were told that this divisive behaviour was a legacy of our turbulent history," my father told me one day, "and that, in time, it would disappear."

Certainly the small communities who had settled in the Lebanese mountains had struggled to survive under the Ottoman regime, where they had been subjected to insults, everyday frustrations, and arbitrary rules, so it was unsurprising that they felt the need for protection. The Maronites turned to France, while their rivals, the Druze, had links with England. Sunni Muslims sought protection from the Turks, Orthodox Christians from the Russians, and so on. The Greek-Catholic community, of which my father was a member, sought refuge under the umbrella of the Austro-Hungarian Empire—and though this connection was largely symbolic, I still remember that an imposing framed portrait of Emperor Franz Joseph hung in one of the houses in our village.

These links offered people a connection to the outside world, or at the very least the feeling that they had not been completely abandoned. And it is undeniable that they had had positive effects, such as encouraging the building of schools and universities. Moreover, they had played a decisive role in the birth of the country.

After the First World War, when the Ottoman Empire began to collapse, the leaders of the Maronite Church argued that France should be given the League of Nations mandate to govern the territory, and should map out the borders of a new state where they could feel at home. This resulted in the creation of Lebanon as it now exists.

In fact, in the early days, many of its citizens thought of it as a French creation designed to favour the Maronites. Some contemporary scholars wondered why France had not created a Greater Syria, or even a larger state regrouping all the Arab peoples.

In this region marked by various different peoples for whom sovereignty was a recent idea, there were always many who supported some form of union. Such plans were probably completely unrealistic. But no more so than deciding to give each of the numerous communities their own sovereign state. And no more so than trying to designate countries created by a hurried cut-and-paste as eternal homelands.

6

The issue of Arab unity took centre stage in the years that followed the rise of Nasser. Having become a hero to the peoples of the region, he resolved to bring them all together into a state that would stretch "from the ocean to the Gulf," eradicating the borders that had been drawn up by colonialists. Crowds enthusiastically cheered the project.

In February 1958, this fervour increased when the Syrian leadership, weary of the chronic instability afflicting their country and aware of their citizens' support for Pan-Arabism, solemnly asked Nasser to take over the reins of power in Syria. A political union was declared: the United Arab Republic, a sovereign state of which Egypt was the "southern province" and Syria the "northern province."

The birth of the UAR was met with rapturous joy in many neighbouring countries. A wave of hope swept through Iraq and Yemen, through Sudan and Morocco, at the thought that Pan-Arabism—long considered a distant dream—was finally becoming a reality. In Beirut and in other Lebanese cities, there were mass demonstrations demanding that the country immediately join the UAR and become the "western province."

I need hardly say that, for my mother's family—having just fled Egypt, its police state, and its punitive policy of nationalization, to seek refuge in Lebanon—the prospect that their adoptive country might become part of Nasser's new republic was greeted with horror. It was as though they were being relentlessly pursued by fate.

My father, as much out of personal conviction as sym-

pathy for my mother's feelings, was alarmed and outraged by what was happening. At that time, he was a
newspaper columnist, whose incisive and sardonic daily
columns had made him a hit with readers. His usual targets were the atavism of his fellow citizens and the follies
of political life. When the United Arab Republic was declared, he unleashed a diatribe: *When a country has the
privilege to be called Egypt, it does not change its name! All
around the world, in the greatest universities, there are eminent scholars who are proud to call themselves Egyptologists!
Should we now call them "UARologists" and demand that dis-
tinguished universities rename their Egyptology departments
"UARology departments"?*

Many of my father's readers laughed heartily. But many
others did not. In fact, he even received death threats. His
friends advised him to temper his words and refrain
from attacking a leader who was idolized by the masses,
lest he be targeted by some fanatic. It is true that feelings
were running high, and tensions had dangerously esca-
lated. In fact, the arguments between the pro-Nasser and
anti-Nasser factions would eventually degenerate into a
civil war. One that, though brief, was bitter and bloody
and left several thousand dead.

I was nine years old, and I have only the haziest memories of what, in the history of my homeland, is referred to
as "the Revolution of '58." What remains engraved in my
memory are the voices of my father and my mother when
they talked about tragic events in front of me: the assassination of a Christian journalist who supported Nasser;
the kidnap and murder of another journalist, also Christian, who was fiercely hostile to Nasser; the torching of
the home of the Prime Minister, one of the few Muslim
politicians who dared to take a stand against the Rais ...
I also remember that the schools were closed for six
months.

On July 14 of that year, when the Iraqi monarchy was overthrown in a bloody coup d'état, when members of the Iraqi royal family and pro-Western leaders were slaughtered in the streets, the US feared that Lebanon would be caught up in the tide of left-wing nationalism sweeping through the Middle East. Within forty-eight hours, they staged a military intervention, landing troops from the US fleet in the Mediterranean, from US bases in Germany; some were even flown in from North Carolina. Fourteen thousand soldiers took part in Operation Blue Bat; they occupied the Port of Beirut, the International Airport, the main streets, and the government buildings. Instantly, fighting between local factions subsided.

To end the crisis, parliament, with the support of Washington, elected a new president, General Fuad Chehab, who was commander of the armed forces. The scion of a princely family that had long governed Mount Lebanon under the Ottomans, he had trained at the Saint-Cyr military academy, and was a staunch admirer of the French republican model of government. He, more than any other Lebanese leader, had a sense of statesmanship and the determination needed to forge a nation. Upon election, he made a speech proclaiming that the bloody events that had rocked the country had produced "neither winners nor losers," and initiated an ambitious project to reconcile opposing factions and provide the country with modern institutions.

One of his first initiatives was a symbolic gesture of great significance, and might have had lasting effects had the country and the region evolved differently: he met with Nasser on the Syrian–Lebanese border, or more precisely in a hut built to straddle the border separating Lebanon from the "northern province" of the UAR.

In this humble corrugated-iron shack, poorly heated

despite the winter chill, the president of a small, divided nation proceeded to negotiate on equal terms with the most powerful and most feared man in the Arab world, and succeeded in reaching a sort of "historic compromise." Chehab pledged that Lebanon would never again serve as a base for Nasser's enemies, and in return, Nasser promised never again to mention Lebanon's accession to the United Arab Republic.

My family were not particularly well-disposed to this compromise. In conversations, they accused the Lebanese president of "aligning" himself with Nasser, of turning the country into a "satellite" of the UAR, and warned that before long we would see newspapers being censored and businesses nationalized.

But these fears proved unwarranted. In hindsight, the meeting in that hut on the border seems like one of the few times when Lebanon intelligently managed to defend its sovereignty and protect itself from the deadly upheavals that racked the region.

*

At dawn on September 28, 1961, there was another coup d'état in Damascus. This time against Nasser, against union with Egypt. The leaders of the coup accused Nasser of treating Syria like a colony, like the spoils of war, and bleeding the country dry. It is true that bureaucratic socialism had proven as ruinous to the economy in Syria as it had in Egypt.

In my family, the breakup of the UAR was greeted with relief, even delight. I still remember the whoops of joy at the news bulletins and the patriotic songs broadcast by Radio Damascus, which was controlled by the leaders of the coup. In his newspaper the following day, my father was so enthusiastic that General Chehab summoned him to the presidential palace for a dressing-down.

The President was worried that the frustration of Nasser's supporters might lead to riots on the streets of Beirut and other Lebanese cities, where the memory of the 1958 events was still raw. It was crucial not to add fuel to the flames, he insisted. Columnists had a duty to be circumspect and responsible. "Since we have got what we wanted, we can at least pretend to be sorry for those who lost," Chehab said with a wry smile. It is a story my father often told, and I never knew whether the use of "we" was merely a turn of phrase, or whether the President wanted to let my father know he shared his feelings.

What is certain is that the union between Syria and Egypt had constituted a real and imminent threat to the independence and the civic peace of Lebanon, and it was only through the wisdom, the foresight, and the skill of its leaders at the time that the country came through the ordeal unscathed, and perhaps even more united.

In the years that followed, two political coalitions emerged: one favourable to President Chehab and his political line was aptly named "the Line"; the other, which opposed him, was called "the Alliance." Both coalitions had Christian and Muslim members who clashed about ideas and policies, not simply about family or religion. The country seemed to have taken the right path, that of a nation resolved to gradually modernize and "secularize" its political life and institutions.

The policy was noble, constructive, exciting, and audacious, and seemed destined to succeed. Lebanon had considerable assets. Its schools and universities, its newspapers, banks, and commercial traditions were the finest in the region. It was a country that prized freedom of expression, it had open relationships with both East and West. It might have lifted up the countries of the Levant and indeed the entire Arab world, drawn them towards greater democracy and modernity. Instead, it found itself dragged down. Towards greater violence and intolerance. Towards poverty and decline. Towards a complete loss of confidence both in itself and in its vision of the future.

1

The sadness I feel at the failure of such a promising model of nationhood is one from which I will never truly recover. Nor do I have the heart to look for facile excuses. The failure can perhaps be explained in part by the crises that wracked the Middle East and presented daunting challenges to my homeland. But the fault lies partly with the disastrous manner in which my country responded to these crises.

In the preceding pages I talked about a crucial moment when our leaders managed to find a good way to extricate our country from a bad situation. This, sadly, was the exception, not the rule. Since independence, and more especially in recent decades, few leaders have demonstrated a sense of statesmanship. Most have been guided only by the interests of their faction, their clan, their religion. It was common practice for them to seek powerful allies beyond the country's borders.

Each community justified its compromises by the fact that they were a minority, that they had suffered for a long time, that they needed to be able to defend themselves at all costs. The fact is that every community in Lebanon, even the largest, is a minority; every community has suffered persecution or humiliation at some point in time; every community has felt the need to use cunning in order to survive. As a result, every community went to great lengths to forge regional and international links with partners of every kind, partners who had their own ambitions, their own fears, their own feuds ...

As the years have passed, bringing new crises, new wars, Lebanon has become a field on which countless battles and proxy battles have been fought: between Russians and Americans, Israelis and Palestinians, Palestinians and Syrians, Syrians and Israelis, Iraqis and Syrians, Iranians and Saudis, Iranians and Israelis—the list is a long one. And every time the foreign antagonists have solicited the aid of one or another of Lebanon's local factions who, citing some excellent pretext, have considered it astute and indeed legitimate to use external forces to advance their own aims, without unduly worrying about the country and its fragile balance.

The walls of my little homeland eventually crumbled, from its elegant roofs to its foundations. Nothing remained of what we had hoped to build, and nothing worked any longer. Political institutions were so rocked by each new election that they were on the brink of collapse. The economy survived only through an endless series of short-term measures that postponed bankruptcy by another few months. Corruption rose to the level of systematic looting; meanwhile the general populace was deprived of basic services such as water, electricity, medical care, public transport, telecommunications, and refuse collection.

This physical and moral decay is all the more distressing given that the Beirut of my childhood was a rare example of peaceful coexistence between religions, one that could, I think, have provided this war-torn region, and other parts of the world, an example to consider.

I am keenly aware that, as we grow older, it is commonplace for people to see their youth as some golden age. Notwithstanding this fact, it seems obvious that today there is nowhere in the world where Christian, Muslim, and Jewish communities live together in peace and harmony.

In predominantly Islamic countries, members of other religions are treated as second-class citizens at best, and frequently as pariahs or scapegoats; a situation that, moreover, has become worse rather than better over time.

In countries founded on the Christian tradition, the attitude towards Islam is characterized by suspicion and mistrust. Not simply because of terrorism. There is an ancient mistrust, one born from the rivalry between two evangelical religions that share the same global ambitions, religions that, for centuries, have clashed in a series of crusades and anti-crusades, conquests and reconquests, colonizations and decolonizations.

As to the relationship between Muslims and Jews, this, too, is characterized by mistrust, a mistrust that stems from a relatively recent but very bitter rivalry between different forms of religious nationalism that are engaged in a total war on every front, around the world.

This profound distrust between followers of the monotheistic religions, which is deeply rooted in people's minds and constantly fuelled by current events, makes any fruitful exchange between populations, or harmony between cultures, all but impossible.

I have no doubt that in this wide world there are countless people of goodwill who sincerely want to understand the Other, to coexist, to overcome their prejudices and their fears. But what we rarely encounter, on the other hand, and what I have only ever experienced in the city where I was born, is that easy-going intimacy between Christians and Jews familiar with Arabic culture and Muslims resolutely turned towards the West, its culture, its lifestyle, and its values.

This vanishingly rare model of coexistence between different religions and cultures was the result, not of some explicit universalist doctrine, but of instinctive, pragmatic wisdom. I remain convinced that it deserved to have a greater influence. There are even times when I believe it might have served as an antidote to many of the poisons of the current century. Or, at the very least, might have provided compelling arguments to those who would resist cultural entrenchment. The fact that the very people who might act as catalysts now find themselves rootless and in danger of extinction is not simply unfortunate for the communities themselves but for cultural diversity. The fragmentation of pluralist societies in the Middle East has caused irreparable moral damage, a damage that affects all human societies, and has unleashed unspeakable barbarity on our world.

*

When it comes to dealing specifically with the way in which religious diversity was managed in the country of my birth, it is difficult to sing its praises, because it ended in failure. But that does not mean we should "throw the baby out with the bathwater," to quote the old maxim.

What I mean by the "baby" here is the idea of acknowledging the existence of all religious communities, even the smallest, of granting them all legal status, freedom of worship, political and cultural rights—in short, granting them dignity. This was a principle adopted by Lebanon at its foundation, one that differentiates it from most other countries.

This policy was long considered little more than a local curiosity, somewhat risible and probably unnecessary, especially given that our neighbours all loudly proclaimed that all their citizens were equal, regardless of religious or ethnic affiliations. Anyone in neighbouring countries who dared suggest that people were treated differently according to whether they were Sunni or Shiite, Muslim or Coptic, Arabic or Kurdish, Alawite and Druze, was accused of spreading lies fabricated by enemies of the state. It was simply not true—we were told—that citizens were treated differently according to their religion or ethnicity in Syria or Iraq, in Egypt or Sudan, in any Arab country, or indeed in non-Arab countries like Israel, Iran, or Turkey! Only in Lebanon did people still use such archaic niceties ...

Today we know that this refusal to acknowledge the existence of different religious and linguistic communities was not intended to bolster equality between citizens or to eradicate discrimination, but precisely the reverse. Everywhere it existed it served only to marginalize and exclude whole populations that had roles they might have played.

In writing these lines, I am thinking primarily about the Middle East, where I was born, a region where no country has reason to be proud of its record. But such denial has not proved to be a virtue elsewhere in the world. While it is theoretically possible that, in certain societies, ways of thinking are sufficiently evolved that it has become superfluous to consider ethnic or religious differences, to be blunt, I know of no such societies. I could not name a single one, though I accept that, in an ideal world, one could exist someday. Until that time, I remain sceptical of those countries which proclaim that all their citizens are treated equally and that no section of the population requires greater protection than the others.

The wish to reassure those communities that had most to fear was present from the beginning of the Lebanese experiment and, to my mind, remains its most remarkable contribution to contemporary civilization. Despite appearances, what others saw as "archaic" actually promised genuine modernity.

But sadly, from the outset, the "baby" was immersed in a "bathwater" that should have been immediately thrown out. By this, I mean *confessionalism*. This term, the regional equivalent of what elsewhere might be called communitarianism, refers to a quota system according to which political and institutional roles are distributed proportionally among religious communities.

The idea in itself was not ridiculous: it was important that, when electing a leader, we were not faced with a Christian candidate opposing a Muslim candidate, each supported by their own co-religionists. As a result, in Lebanon, it was decided that responsibilities should be equally distributed between the different communities. The President would always be a Maronite Christian; the President of the Council, a Sunni Muslim; the Speaker of Parliament a Shia Muslim. In government, there would always be the same number of Christian and Muslim ministers. And each community was to have parliamentary seats that could not be contested. There was even an attempt to impose such quotas in the civil service.

If such a structure was complex, not to say convoluted, it served a purpose and it might indeed have produced the anticipated results; but this was to underestimate the insidious, toxic nature of all quota systems. The hope had been that reducing competition between different communities would gradually reduce tensions between citizens and reinforce a sense of belonging to a nation rather than a religion. But what actually happened was the reverse. Rather than looking to government to defend their rights, citizens found it easier to go through the leaders of their religious communities. These gradually became autonomous satrapies ruled by clans or militias, who put their personal interests above the national interest.

Truth be told—and I write this in the twilight years of my life, and with infinite sadness—rather than keeping the baby and throwing out the dirty bathwater, the opposite happened. We threw out the baby and kept the dirty water. Everything that had seemed promising was stunted from birth. All those things that had seemed worrying and unhealthy, which we hoped were temporary, became more firmly entrenched.

Nowadays, I believe that the ideal solution—both for my native land, and for others—does not lie in a system of quotas, which keep society constrained by a perverse logic, a logic that leads to precisely the result we hoped to avoid; nor in refusing to acknowledge differences, which simply masks problems and often further aggravates them; but in constant vigilance, by which the government constantly ensures that no sector of the population, and ideally no citizen, suffers unfair discrimination based on colour, religion, ethnicity, age, gender, etc. If we are to avoid the gradual decay of the social fabric, and if we refuse to engage with the insidious logic of communitarianism, we must strive to take into account the various sensitivities that exist within the population, such that every citizen can see him- or herself reflected in that society, its social systems, its institutions. This is something that requires a day-to-day vigilance regarding tensions and biases.

Needless to say, it is not that simple. Just as it is not a simple matter for the government of any modern country to manage public health services, transportation, and education. But when we take into account that what is at stake is the very survival of the nation, its prosperity, its place in the world, its civic peace, we owe it to ourselves to find the means, no matter the cost.

*

Am I right to focus on the region where I was born, on its sociological particularities, on the tragedies that have plunged it into grief?

I have chosen to do so because, in recent years, the turmoil within the Arab-Muslim world has become a source of major concern for all humanity. It seems obvious that something serious, something unparalleled, has happened in this region, something that has unsettled our whole world, and turned it from the path it should have taken.

It is almost as though we have all suffered a powerful mental earthquake, whose epicentre lies somewhere near the place where I was born. And it is precisely because I was born and grew up on this "fault line" that I am trying to understand how the quake occurred, and why the aftershocks have spread around the world, with the calamitous consequences now familiar to us all.

I will later return to this subject that has haunted me, one that is the heart of this book. The reason I mention it here, at the end of a chapter about the lost paradise of my childhood, is because it now seems to me that if the experiments in the Levant had succeeded, if they had offered viable social models, then Arab and Muslim societies might have evolved very differently. Towards less obscurantism, less fanaticism, less anguish, less despair ...

Perhaps humanity as a whole would have taken a different path to the one it now finds itself on, one that has led us to the brink of disaster.

II

Of Peoples on the Road to Ruin

The most civilized empires will always as be close to
barbarism as the most polished iron is to rust; nations,
like metals, shine only on their surface.

Antoine de Rivarol (1753–1801)
On Modern Philosophy

1

I have always felt a great attachment for the culture of my parents, I hoped that I might see it be reborn, grow, blossom, regain its influence, its greatness, its generosity, its inventiveness, so that it might once again dazzle all mankind. I never believed that, in my later years, I would find myself describing its path using words such as anguish, despair, disorientation, cataclysm, decline, collapse, ruin ...

But what other words are there to describe the ruined landscape we see stretching away before us? Its countries disintegrating, its ancient communities being uprooted, its magnificent relics destroyed, its cities ravaged, to say nothing of the rise of a savagery beyond words—stonings, beheadings, amputations, crucifixions, lynchings —all dutifully filmed and streamed, so that the rest of the world does not miss a single detail?

Rarely in the history of civilizations has self-loathing led to such extremes. Rather than enhancing the prestige of their civilization, rather than contributing to the human experience through mathematics, architecture, medicine, or philosophy, rather than reminding their contemporaries of the glory days of Cordoba, Granada, Fez, Alexandria, Sirte, Baghdad, Damascus, or Aleppo, the heirs to the great builders of yesteryear prove themselves unworthy of the very traditions of which they are custodians. One might go so far as to say they are deliberately trying to shame those who love their civilization, to vindicate their harshest critics.

Time was when those who despised Arabs were accused of xenophobia and colonialist nostalgia; these days, everyone feels entitled to hate Arabs in the name of modernity, secularism, freedom of expression, and the rights of women.

I spoke of "self-loathing"—this is something that strikes me as relatively recent. The trait I most associate with my people, one that constantly frustrated me as a young man, was their lack of confidence both in themselves and in their ability to take control of their destiny. It is a mindset not unrelated to self-loathing; indeed, it is probably fertile soil for self-loathing to thrive in. But it does not have the same destructive consequences, nor is it the preserve of a single people, ethnic group, or religious community. Any group that has long suffered the brutal authority of colonialism, of an occupying force, of a powerful city, will recognise the feeling of dependence, the need to seek approval from a higher authority, the fear of seeing its decisions scorned, penalized, invalidated.

In this regard, the history of my homeland speaks for itself. For centuries, all orders came from Istanbul, from the Sublime Porte, as we used to say. From time to time, some emir in the mountains would rebel, carve out a fiefdom, forge alliances, win two or three skirmishes. Alas, the Sublime Porte eventually retaliated; the rebel was defeated, arrested, and taken in shackles to some dank dungeon. It was only in the dying days of the Ottoman Empire that Mount Lebanon was able to escape its grip, when there were sovereign powers who ruled through the Sultan according to their own interests.

But the habit of obeying the orders of the Sublime Porte did not simply disappear. Although orders no longer came from Istanbul, people expected them from Washington, from Moscow, from Paris or London; and from capitals in the region: Cairo, Damascus, Tehran, or Riyadh. Even today, when Lebanon elects a new president, for example, voters do not ask themselves which candidate would be best for the country, but rather who the various ambassadors will favour; more than once it has happened that the results of an election have been delayed beyond constitutional deadlines, while voters waited for the "electoral powers" to come to an agreement.

If the situation in Lebanon has its peculiarities, it is nonetheless typical of a mindset that can be found to varying degrees in all Arab countries, one characterised by an undue regard for what the "Powers that be" might want. Voters believe that these Powers are omnipotent, that it is futile to resist, that these Powers work together and hence it is impossible to play them off against each other. Moreover, voters believe that these Powers have plans for the future of nations, plans that cannot be changed and at which they can only guess; as a result, even the most anodyne statement from a junior White House advisor is pored over as though it were a heavenly decree.

This failing, which is common to my people, is the result of a lengthy experience of disillusionment and resignation. Why bother to protest, demand, rebel, when we know that it can only end in a bloodbath? Why wage war against this opponent or that dynasty when the Powers will never abandon them? And obviously, these are the very Powers that decide when war begins, and when it ends ... Anyone who doubts this accepted wisdom is seen as naive or ignorant.

*

However foolish and frustrating, this lack of confidence still seems benign when compared to what has emanated from the Arab world in recent years, namely a deep loathing, both of themselves and of others, together with a glorification of death and of suicidal behaviour.

It is difficult to explain in words such a monstrous drift. All I wish to say here is that, to those born at the same time and in the same region as me, this development seems at once more disturbing and less surprising than it does to most of our contemporaries.

When a man decides to take his own life, all one can do is wonder why he felt pushed to such extremes. Although the reasons why someone chooses to commit suicide may differ, there is usually a common factor: a sense of hopelessness, of having irrevocably lost that without which life is not worth living—health, wealth, dignity, or a loved one.

I am not about to say that the same is true of nations and peoples. That is something that never happens. Yes, it is true that a group of people—a family, a gang, a minor sect—commits mass suicide from time to time. Ancient chronicles report that even in Phoenicia, in the fourth century BC, the citizens of Sidon, besieged by the Persian king, set their city ablaze, preferring to die rather than surrender to the invader; and everyone knows the Siege of Masada, where Jewish Sicarii rebels committed suicide to avoid falling into the hands of the Roman legionaries.

But the phenomenon we are witnessing in this century goes beyond that. The idea that millions of people are in the grip of despair, that many have embraced a suicidal attitude, is something that has never been seen before in history, and I believe that we are not yet aware of the scale of what is unfolding before our eyes throughout the Arab-Muslim world, and in the countries of the diaspora.

I remember watching the nascent Syrian uprising in April 2011, footage shot at night in which demonstrators marched, and chanted: "We are going to heaven, martyrs in our millions!" A slogan soon echoed in other countries throughout the region.

I watched these men with as much fascination as horror. They showed great courage, especially given that they were unarmed while the supporters of the regime opened fire at every demonstration. But these words revealed damaged souls, they laid bare the anguish of the world.

When a person loses the will to live, it falls to those closest to him to give him hope. When whole populations allow themselves to be overcome by the urge to destroy and to destroy themselves, it falls to all of us, their contemporaries, their peers, to find a solution. If not out of solidarity with the Other, at least out of a desire to survive.

Because in the era in which we live, despair can sweep across oceans, scale walls, cross any frontier, physical or mental, and it is not easily contained.

2

I constantly keep with me, written on a folded card stock, the words of a little-known Arab poet, Abu al-Salt, born in Dénia, Spain, in the eleventh century:

If I am made of clay,
The world entire is my country
And all its creatures are my kin.

In fact, it is not necessary to go back so far in time to see a different face of the civilization of my forefathers. The atrocity we see unfurling before us now is more recent than it seems. The reality I personally experienced was very different. But these days, when I talk about it, I feel in those around me a mounting sense of irritation, impatience, and disbelief.

Not that I find this really surprising. Once a calamity has occurred, it is impossible to prove that it might have been avoided. Even if one personally believes that it could have been. Which I do. I spent my youth in this part of the world, and ever since have constantly observed. It has been the dubious privilege of my generation to witness the slow metamorphosis of Dr. Jekyll into Mr. Hyde; by which I mean the transformation of a vast group of peoples typical of their era, people who shared the dreams, ambitions, and illusions of their contemporaries, into frenzied, raging, intimidating, desperate crowds.

This "normality" has long since been forgotten. Many people find it difficult to believe it ever existed, accustomed as they now are to seeing anything related to Arabs or to Islam as hailing from another galaxy. So it is worth reminding them, for example, that the ideological fault line between Marxism and its rivals that divided humanity in the twentieth century ran through the Arab-Muslim world just as it did the rest of the planet.

Countries like Sudan, Yemen, Iraq, and Syria had significant communist movements. Indeed, the Gaza Strip was ruled by a Marxist–Leninist organization until 1990, when it became a stronghold of Hamas, the Palestinian offshoot of the Muslim Brotherhood.

Indonesia is an even more illuminating example. These days, it is invariably referred to as the largest Muslim country in the world. When I was a teenager, Indonesia was equally famous for having the largest communist party in the world after China and the Soviet Union, a party that, at its peak, comprised nearly three million members, slightly more than its closest "rival," the Italian Communist Party.

I'm not seeking to praise communism. It raised great hopes for the whole of humanity, only to betray them. It gathered together people of staunch principles, people of great generosity, and led them into a dead end. Its failure was cataclysmic, as were its aberrations, and it paved the way for the global decay we are witnessing today.

If there is still a note of nostalgia when I talk about the recent past, it is because the existence of an unambiguously secular ideology like Marxism in many Islamic nations between the 1920s and the late 1980s now seems to me to be a significant and illuminating phenomenon, and one whose disappearance can legitimately be regretted.

Leaving aside the purely political, it is worth remembering the intellectual and cultural atmosphere that prevailed for much of the twentieth century, and that I personally experienced in Beirut. I am thinking, for example, of the discussions University of Khartoum students used to have in the gardens of Mosul or the cafés of Aleppo; of the Gramsci books they used to read, the Brecht plays they performed and applauded; of the poems of Nâzim Hikmet and Paul Éluard; the revolutionary songs that made their hearts beat faster; the world events that incited them to action—the Vietnam War, the assassination of Patrice Lumumba, the imprisonment of Nelson Mandela, Yuri Gagarin's space flight, the death of "Che" Guevara. More than that, I feel a profound nostalgia when I remember the smiles of female students from Afghanistan or Yemen that shine out from the photographs of the 1960s. Then I think of the cramped, gloomy, sad, and stunted universe of the young men and women of today who visit those same places, walk those same streets, sit in those same lecture halls.

There are other reasons for my sadness, reasons that I rarely talk about, though I think about them often.

When I recall the history of the region where I was born over the past century, I realize that it was only in the Marxist-inspired political movements that, for a time, Muslims, Jews, and Christians of all denominations could come together. It is true that in most countries the impact of these movements was limited. However, there were some notable exceptions.

I am thinking in particular about a character known as "Comrade Fahd." Born in Baghdad in 1901 to an Assyrian Christian family, he was educated in an American missionary school before discovering Marxism and becoming involved in the social struggle. He was gifted with such extraordinary charisma and such keen organizational skills that he not only became the undisputed leader of the nascent Iraqi Communist Party, but one of the most popular figures in the country, across all communities. The government had him imprisoned, but even from his prison cell, he continued to organize general strikes and mass demonstrations. So, they decided to get rid of him once and for all. He was court-martialled and sentenced to death for "contacts with a foreign state," "acts of sedition," and "the propagation of communism among the armed forces," and, in February 1949, was hanged in the public square.

They say that the whole nation was plunged into mourning. His comrades were inconsolable, and thousands of activists vowed to avenge his death. It is even said that when the Iraqi monarchy was overthrown, nine years later, protesters seized the officials they believed were responsible for his death, and dragged them from the royal palace to the place where "Comrade Fahd" had been executed so they would suffer the same fate.

I tell this story merely to point out that, these days, there is not a single political movement in Iraq, nor in the rest of the region, that would have as its leader someone from a minority community like the Assyrian Christians. Any Iraqi promoted to a position of leadership must necessarily come from one of the three major communities—Shiites, Sunnis, or Kurds. In fact, there is not a single political party that comprises members from all three groups ...

As for Assyrian Christians or Chaldean Catholics, they were forced to flee Mesopotamia, where their ancestors had lived for thousands of years, to seek exile in America, Canada, Sweden, and elsewhere. They were uprooted, only yesterday, before our very eyes, to the general indifference that has characterized this century.

*

The case of "Comrade Fahd" raises an issue that has pre-occupied me for some time, one that has become more important with the recent rise of communitarianism, and one that is little discussed.

I have often wondered whether there has been an implicit message in the history of communism from its outset, one that has been promulgated, consciously or unconsciously, by its founders, its adherents, and its critics, one that might be formulated as follows: it is not only to the *proletarians* that Marx promised salvation, but also to the *minoritarians*, all those who could not fully identify with the nation to which they supposedly belonged. That, in any case, is how many have understood his message.

It is no coincidence that the first leader of the Iraqi Communist Party was a Christian, and that the first leader of the Syrian Communist Party was a Kurd. It is no coincidence that so many Jews from Russia, Germany, Poland, Romania, and beyond enthusiastically joined the movement. Nor is it a coincidence that, after the foundation of the State of Israel, the Arabs who chose to remain rallied en masse to the flag of the Communist Party: it was the only movement that allowed them to participate in political life on the same terms as their Jewish fellow citizens without feeling they were betraying their Arab identity. In many countries, those who do not belong to the dominant religion or ethnic majority find themselves excluded, or at the very least marginalized; if they wish to engage in politics, they must join a movement where they have a chance to feel they are on equal terms with compatriots from the majority communities.

Marxist-inspired movements have long played this role in the Levant, in Eastern Europe, and in many other parts of the world. Such movements drew people from different faiths and backgrounds, all of them attracted by a philosophy that focused on *class* and thereby glossed over the handicap, not to say the curse of being part of a minority. Here was an opportunity to transcend their narrow religious affiliations by becoming part of a vast identity, one that embraced "the proletariat of all countries," that is to say all of humanity; what more could they hope for? Irrespective of the political ideas that accompanied the movement, this mindset unquestionably represented progress, and not simply for activists themselves; in rising above their own narrow communities, they were freeing themselves from the rigid logic of communitarianism and making their society a little freer in the process.

It seems clear that most of these people would have been outraged if someone had explained the subconscious reasons of their commitment in such terms. From their point of view, they were simply rebelling against oppression, against alienation, against man's exploitation of man. They were happy to talk about their solidarity with the working class, about their class consciousness; some even proudly referred to themselves as "traitors" to the bourgeoisie into which they had been born. But they would have found it difficult to admit that their religion or their ethnicity had anything to do with their struggle.

I was briefly one of their number. So briefly that it would be presumptuous for me to devote more than a few lines to that period. I joined the movement when I was eighteen and a half; I was nineteen and a half when I left it. I quickly realized that I did not have the temperament of an activist or of a follower. So, I tiptoed away, with no fuss, no qualms, no acrimony. Without breaking with any of the friends who were still part of the movement, and retaining only those beliefs that already dovetailed with my earliest convictions, by which I mean the belief in a world where no human suffers discrimination because of colour, religion, language, nationality, gender, or social background.

Perhaps these—universalist, or simply conciliatory—beliefs were deeply rooted in me because I was a member of a tiny community within a tiny country; those with profiles similar to mine thrive in certain environments, and wither in others. That said, I have been careful not to infer that such a mindset comes naturally to those in a minority. The most instinctive reaction of those in a minority is to assert their identity and embrace it rather than attempting to transcend it. This has always been true; in this century, it has simply become more so.

I have talked about nostalgia and regret. These vague notions merit closer scrutiny. Would Arab or Muslim countries have evolved better if the communist parties there had played a more important role? I do not think so, in fact I am convinced that the opposite is true. Just look at how Communist regimes have acted when they rose to power. It is reasonable to assume that, rather than miracles, we would have witnessed monstrous abuses—pogroms, massacres, the emergence of a host of tin-pot Stalins. From this point of view, there is no reason for regret.

What can be regretted, however, is the disappearance of the only political forum that offered any citizen, regardless of their ethnic or religious background, an opportunity to play a leading role in their country.

I would happily have accepted it had the space provided by Marxism on the left of the political spectrum been replaced by something comparable on the right. But that is not what happened. This space simply disappeared. The minority have once again become outcasts, and potential victims. This, to my mind, represents an irretrievable loss, in fact a disastrous regression. Both for the region where I was born and for the rest of the world.

Since I myself was a member of such a minority, I may be giving the impression that I am merely thinking of my own interests. But what I find worrying is something very different. Throughout human history, the manner in which a society treats its minorities has been indicative of the larger problems that affect every citizen, and every aspect of that country's social and political life. The Nazis' treatment of the Jews in the 1930s and 1940s was disastrous and deadly for Germany as a whole, and beyond. In a society where minorities face discrimination and persecution, everything becomes warped and corrupted. Concepts become meaningless. To carry on talking about elections, debate, academic freedom, or the rule of law becomes inappropriate and deceptive.

When it becomes impossible for people to exercise their civic rights without reference to their ethnicity or religion, then the country as a whole is on the path to barbarism. For, as long as a member of a minority community can play a role on the national stage, it indicates that a country prizes the concepts of humanity and citizenship above all others. When this is no longer true, it means that the very concepts of citizenship and of humanity have failed. This is now the case in every country of the Levant, without exception. And it is increasingly true, in varying degrees, in other parts of the world.

Even in countries with strong democratic traditions, it is becoming increasingly difficult to fully participate as a citizen without reference to one's ethnic origins, religion, or particular affiliations.

In a lecture to his students, the American philosopher William James posed a pertinent question: since wartime mobilizes people and elicits what is best in human beings—*esprit de corps*, mutual aid, passion, self-sacrifice—should we, as others do, hope for a "good war" to put an end to idleness and laxity? His response was that societies needed to create a "moral equivalent of war," that is to say peaceful struggles that would appeal to the same virtues, mobilize as much energy, without tending towards the atrocities that trigger wars. I am tempted here to make a similar observation: perhaps what is needed in this century is a "moral equivalent" of proletarian internationalism but without the accompanying atrocities. Surely, faced with the explosion of Identitarianism, it would be good to see the emergence of a broad movement capable of rallying our contemporaries around universal values, beyond all religious, ethnic, or cultural political boundaries?

Here, too, the region where I was born might have set an example, might have spread light across the world, but in the end, sadly, it spread only darkness.

3

This brief digression about the chequered history of Marxism was principally intended as a reminder of the "normality" of the Arab world, a way of underscoring that it long cherished the same dreams and the same illusions as the rest of the planet. I felt I needed to emphasize this point, since the prevailing view of the Arab world today is precisely that of fundamental "Otherness." People now believe that, since the dawn of time, it has harboured "irreconcilable differences." They have even come to think of it, consciously or subconsciously, as a different world, inhabited by a different kind of humanity.

It is a view widely held by an increasingly large group of people who feel distrust or hostility towards the Arab-Muslim world and the peoples who have come from there; by militant Islamists, whose words and actions are designed to reinforce this perception; and by a wide range of people from all backgrounds and faiths who are disturbed by certain actions, who see these actions as different from their own behaviour, and in good faith, draw what they consider to be the obvious conclusions.

I find such attitudes worrying because, whether we like it or not, the belief in "irreconcilable differences" is a slippery slope that ultimately leads to rejecting the notion of universality, and even of humanity. It is to counter such beliefs that I constantly point out that the Arab world of my youth shared the same goals as the rest of the world. That world shared the same concerns, the same discussions, the same laughter. And it might just as easily have evolved into something very different from what we see today.

Anyone like me who enjoys browsing the internet can find an amazing sequence filmed in Egypt in the mid-1960s. Though it is in Arabic, other internet users have subtitled it in various languages, including French and English. In the clip, we see Nasser in a lecture hall or a conference room, explaining to the audience his qualms with the Muslim Brotherhood. What is interesting about the documentary is not simply what the Rais says, but the reactions of the audience.

The President explains that, after the overthrow of the Egyptian monarchy, the Muslim Brotherhood tried to control the nascent revolution, and that he had personally met their supreme leader to try to find some common ground. "Do you know what he demanded? That I impose the wearing of the hijab in Egypt, that any woman should cover her head before stepping out into the street!"

The hall is rocked by a burst of laughter. From the audience comes a voice that suggests that the leader of the Muslim Brotherhood should wear the veil. More laughter. Nasser carries on. "I said to him 'Are you trying to take us back to the time of Caliph al-Hakim, who decreed that people should not venture into the street at night, and should shut themselves away by day?' But the leader of the Brotherhood insisted: 'You are the President, you should decree that all women must cover themselves.' I said: 'You have a daughter who is studying at the medical school, and she does not wear the veil. You cannot force the veil on one woman, who is your own daughter, but you would have me go down into the streets to impose the veil on ten million Egyptian women?'"

The Rais is so amused by his story that he struggles to carry on with his speech. He takes a sip of water. When he finally manages to overcome his fit of giggles, he lists the demands made by the Islamist leader: women should no longer be allowed to work, all cinemas and theatres should be shut down, etc. "In other words, darkness should reign everywhere!" Another burst of laughter ...

Arabs who watch this footage half a century later no longer feel like laughing. It makes them want to cry. Because it is unthinkable that an Arab leader would make such a speech today, or treat wearing the veil as a joke, when so many people think of it as a tragedy. On the other hand, it is a safe bet that all the women who attended that lecture, if they are still alive, and the daughters and granddaughters of the men who were in the audience, are all now demurely veiled. Sometimes by choice, and sometimes because social pressure gives them no choice.

I need hardly remind the reader that we are not talking about an ordinary politician, or the leader of some radical secularist faction, but the man who was, by far, the most popular leader of Arab world and the entire Muslim world. His portrait hung everywhere: in Beirut, in Cairo, and also in Algiers, in Nouakchott, in Aden, in Baghdad, and in cities as distant as Karachi and Kuala Lumpur. Nasser was the leader who was expected to restore the dignity of his people. Since his death, no one has so far succeeded in taking his place in people's hearts.

As I was writing these pages, I called to ask my mother to clarify some details, and once again she talked to me about Egypt as it used to be, about the beaches in Alexandria, the horseback rides, about "our" house in Heliopolis. In her memories, Nasser does not come off in a good light. If I can talk about him with a certain nostalgia, it is because I compare his era, not to the one that preceded it, which I never really knew, but to the era that followed—our era. And the contrast is striking. Nasser might have been a military dictator, a somewhat xeno-phobic nationalist, and—as far as my family were con-cerned—a despoiler, yet the fact remains that, in his time, the Arab world was respected. It was driven by a project, it had not yet descended into the despair and self-loathing I described earlier.

*

I have just cited the veil as an example; here is another, one that concerns the two major branches of Islam, Sunni and Shia.

These days, the relationship is marked by bitter vio-lence. A bloodthirsty violence that results in indiscrimi-nate massacres in which mosques are targeted during prayer or people are targeted while engaged in pilgrim-age. To say nothing of the brutal verbal abuse; five min-utes on the internet is enough to get a sense of the obscene, insulting terms they use when they talk about each other—a violence that people describe as "secular." But Nasser, a Sunni Muslim like most people in Egypt, was married to the daughter of an Iranian merchant living in Alexandria. His wife, born Tahia Kazem, was a Shia Muslim, but in those days, nobody cared, neither the president's supporters nor his detractors. The ancient, bitter feud between the two main branches of Islam seemed to be a thing of the past.

Marriages between Shia and Sunni Muslims had be-come common in the Lebanon of my youth. Indeed, mar-riages between Muslims and Christians had also risen. Doubtless they continued to arouse misgivings in vari-ous sections of the media, but more and more families accepted them without making a fuss, as a natural devel-opment in a changing world.

I still remember a grand middle-class Muslim lady who came to visit me one day. I was only twenty-five years old, but I must have seemed to her like a wise old man. Her daughter was dating a friend of mine, a Christian university student, and they planned to marry. "I realize that my coming to you is unusual," she told me, "but I just want you to tell me, in confidence, whether you think he is a serious young man, and whether you think he will make her happy. It is not easy for us to give our daughter's hand to someone from another religion; it will cause tension, and I need to be sure that this young man is worth it, so that I do not regret taking this step later."

At the time, I was deeply touched by her words. Today, they seem to me to epitomize the Levantine civilization that I so loved.

Do the examples I have just given mean that the Arab world was quietly heading towards modernity, secularism, and civil peace when "historical events" turned it from this path and pushed it in a very different direction? Things are not so simple. Over several centuries, the society my parents knew had been marked by shortcomings, contradictions, and weaknesses that prevented it from meeting the challenges it faced; to return to the metaphor I already mentioned, one might say that there was always a possibility that Dr. Jekyll would turn into Mr. Hyde.

But this is true of all people, all nations, all civilizations: under certain circumstances, the monstrous creature takes over, and the noble doctor is eclipsed. In the last century, people helplessly wondered how the country of Goethe, Beethoven, and Lessing could come to be identified with Goering, Himmler, and Goebbels.

Fortunately, Germany has been able to turn the page, to return to its true heroes, its true values, and now offers Europe and the rest of the world the very model of a mature democracy. Dare I hope that the people who gave birth to Averroes, to Avicenna, to Ibn Arabi, to Omar Khayyam, and to the Emir Abdelkader, might one day learn to return to the great glories of its civilization?

4

For years, I have contemplated the Arab world with dread, forcing myself to try and understand how it could have suffered such a decline. Opinions on the subject are endless and contradictory. Some blame violent radicalism, blind jihadism, and, more broadly, the ambiguous relationship between religion and politics in the Islamic world; others blame colonialism, the greed and insensitivity of the West, US hegemony, or the Israeli occupation of Palestinian territories. All though all of these factors have certainly played a role, no single factor explains the drift that we are currently witnessing.

There is, however, I believe, one event that stands out from all the rest, one that marks a decisive turning point in the history of the region and beyond; a military conflict that took place in an incredibly short space of time, but whose effects were to prove long-lasting: I am talking about the Arab–Israeli war of June 1967.

How can I describe its impact? The comparison that spontaneously comes to mind is the bombing of Pearl Harbor—but only for the breathtaking intensity of the Japanese aerial attack, and the element of surprise, not for its military consequences. For although the US fleet suffered heavy losses in terms of men and artillery on the morning of December 7, 1941, the country retained much of its defensive and offensive capabilities. Whereas on the morning of June 5, 1967, the air forces of Egypt, Syria, and Jordan were virtually annihilated; their armies were forced to retreat, yielding significant territory to the Israelis: the Old City of Jerusalem, the West Bank, the Golan Heights, the Gaza Strip, and the Sinai Peninsula.

Seen from this viewpoint, it might be more appropriate

to compare the Arab defeat with the fall of France in June 1940. The French Army, still wreathed in glory from winning the Great War twenty-two years earlier, quickly collapsed in the face of the German offensive. Roads filled with refugees, Paris was captured, and much of the country occupied. The nation felt dazed, humiliated, violated—feelings that only began to fade after the Liberation, four years later.

The crucial difference between the war of 1967 and these two episodes from the Second World War is that, unlike the Americans and the French, the Arabs dwelt on this defeat, and never again regained their self-confidence.

Half a century has passed since then, as I write these lines, yet things have not improved. One might even say they are still getting worse. Rather than healing and scarring, these wounds became infected, and the world has suffered as a result.

The person who suffered the greatest defeat was Nasser. Until the war, he had enjoyed immense popularity throughout the Arab and the Muslim worlds, to such an extent that his rivals, particularly the Islamist movements, rarely dared attack him openly. Moreover, he was young. He came to power at the age of thirty; he reached the peak of international fame by thirty-eight; in 1967 he was only forty-nine, and everyone believed that he would be in power for a long time to come.

I was eighteen when the war broke out. For weeks, everyone had known it was looming, and had speculated about the likely outcome. The more bullish of those in the Arab world were convinced that Egyptian forces, heavily armed by the Soviets, would make short work of the Israeli Army; they supported this view by quoting anguished statements from the Jewish state claiming it was threatened with annihilation. The more realistic at the time believed it would be a long and painful war in which the Arabs might eventually prevail, if only by virtue of sheer numbers.

Certainly, excepting a few officers in the Israeli General Staff, no one could imagine what would actually happen: a swift and massive air attack that, within hours, would destroy the grounded air forces of Egypt, Syria, and Jordan, making any Arab counter-offensive impossible; then, the following day, the Egyptian commander made the absurd decision to order ground troops to withdraw from the Sinai peninsula, which merely aggravated the debacle.

In less than a week, the fighting was over. Israel and the West immediately dubbed the conflict the "Six-Day War"—a name Arabs have always found insulting; they prefer to call it "The June War" or "Sixty-Seven," or "*Naksa*," a term used by Nasser himself after the defeat to minimize the significance of what had just happened; *naksa* means "setback" or "temporary defeat"; it is more usually used to refer to accidents from which the patient is expected to recover.

But the "patient" in this case never recovered. The Arabs never took their revenge, never managed to overcome the trauma of defeat; and Nasser never again recovered his international stature. He died three years later, at the age of fifty-two. His successors as head of state—Sadat, Mubarak, and the others—did not have Nasser's ambitions, his worldview, or his charisma, nor did they win the affection of the masses. And all those who claimed to replace Nasser in the role of hero of the Arab world, like Saddam Hussein or Muammar Gaddafi, were seen as charlatans.

What was to prove much more significant was that Arab nationalism, until then the dominant ideology in that part of the world, had, overnight, lost all credibility. At first, Marxism–Leninism benefited. But only in certain circles, and only for a brief period, because communism was about to enter its own zone of turbulence and it, too, would lose its appeal.

Ultimately, the true beneficiary of Nasser's defeat was political Islamism. It came to replace nationalism as the dominant ideology in the region. It would replace Nasserism and its avatars as the standard-bearer of patriotic aspirations and would supplant Marxist-inspired movements as the champion of the poor and the oppressed.

*

In seeing this brief war as the cause of the recent political drift in the region where I was born, am I perhaps guilty of the ordinary, commonplace human fallacy of ascribing undue significance to events that we have personally witnessed? For many experts on the Arab world, the descent into hell did not begin with the defeat suffered in 1967, but with that suffered in 1948, which led to the foundation of the State of Israel; and to some, earlier still, with the end of First World War, when the victorious allied powers reneged on the promise made by Colonel T. E. Lawrence to the Sharif of Mecca to create a single, unified Arab state.

Each of these assessments contains a sliver of truth. It is certainly true that frustration among the Arab nations goes back generations, indeed centuries. Nonetheless, if seeking to find the root of the suicidal, murderous despair we see today, the most important date is 1967. Until that point, while the Arabs were certainly angry, they still had hope. In the figure of Nasser in particular. After that date, all hope was lost.

I am almost tempted to set it down in black and white: Arab despair was born on Monday, June 5, 1967.

On that fateful day, I was a young sociology student beginning my end-of-year exams at the École des Lettres in Beirut. I had gone into the exam hall at 8:00 a.m., having listened to the morning news; according to the radio, diplomatic efforts were underway to prevent an armed conflict. When I came out, shortly before noon, a close friend rushed over to me waving a newspaper whose front-page headline announced in huge type that war had broken out, and that the Israeli air force had been destroyed.

Yes, the Israeli air force. All of the newspapers published the same story, which was based on military communiqués between Cairo and Damascus. The air force of every major Arabic country had already been wiped out, but we did not know this, in fact we believed precisely the opposite. Arab radio stations trumpeted the news that the Israeli military had "fallen into the trap," and reeled off the number of planes shot down. Later, these same students would weep tears of shame and rage, but, in that moment, they were busy calculating how many planes the Israelis might still have. A day earlier, the Israeli fleet had numbered three hundred, someone said, of which two hundred and fifty-seven had been destroyed, leaving Israel with only forty bombers, which would soon suffer the same fate.

At home, I repeated this piece of "news" to my father. He nodded, but did not express an opinion. I felt a little disappointed. As a journalist, he fervently followed the news, hour by hour, he regularly talked about current events in his newspaper columns, at the dinner table, and in conversations with me. I could not understand why he seemed so placid in the face of such a momentous event.

In the early evening, he came to me to talk about the planes. He sat down next to me, took out a pack of local cigarettes, the white cardboard box of which he used to scribble notes on. He handed it to me and said simply: "These are the real figures." And, while making every effort not to offend me, he told me that the outcome was precisely the reverse of what the Arabic radio stations had been saying. We would have to be very careful in the coming days, he added. "When people find out what really happened, they will be furious, they'll want to smash everything."

And he was right: the following day, riots broke out in Beirut, in Tripoli, and in a number of other cities in the region. People attacked anything and anyone they thought was an enemy of Nasser and the Arab nation— British companies, American missions, but also Jewish communities, even those as in Tunis who had never been targeted before.

On Friday, Nasser took to the radio to make a solemn, poignant speech in which he conceded defeat and announced his resignation. Millions of people immediately took to the streets in Egypt, in Lebanon, and elsewhere pleading with him to remain in power. The following day, Saturday, he relented.

Most historians believed that his brief "resignation" was merely an astute stratagem so that the masses would pledge their confidence and restore his legitimacy. This is probably true. There is certainly no question that said masses remained loyal to him, and took some comfort in his continued role as head of state.

Although I personally had a thousand reasons to dislike the great man, his resignation left me as devastated as I have ever felt in my life. I had never considered him a father figure yet, suddenly, I felt orphaned. I felt as though I was in the raging torrent, and he was the only branch I could cling to. This, I imagine, is how peoples react when they feel completely helpless.

One particular incident remains engraved in my memory. That year, my first at university, I had enrolled in two separate institutions. At the École des Lettres, I was studying sociology—but the exam I sat on the morning of June 5 would never be corrected, and the remainder of the exams were postponed. At the Université de Saint-Joseph, where I was studying economics, the exams had taken place some weeks before the war, and the results were to be posted on Friday, June 9.

By sheer coincidence, this was the day on which Nasser resigned. So I listened to his speech, broadcast from Cairo on *Sawt al Arab* (Voice of the Arabs), and was so unsettled—by what he said, by his resignation, by the debacle, by everything that was going on—that I forgot about my exams. Only when my mother asked if I had my results did I finally go to get them.

I went down to the university. Posted on noticeboards inside were alphabetical lists of students followed by their grades. I went up to the board. I looked. Then I left.

I was already halfway home when I had the strangest experience: I simply could not remember whether I had passed or failed. I had to go back to look again.

To this day, I have never again experienced such a mental blank. How, in the space of five minutes, was it possible to forget whether I had failed or been admitted to the second year? How could I have forgotten something that was so important to me, and so easy to remember? This momentary blank remains in my memory as a symbol of how harrowing the debacle of June 1967 was for me, and for the Arab world.

I have no doubt that this lapse stemmed from my subconscious need to be part of the despair that had engulfed the city where I was born.

5

The Arabs had lost the war; Israel had won. Nonetheless, in hindsight, I cannot help but wonder whether, ultimately, this brief conflict was not a disaster for all involved. Not in the same sense, it goes without saying, nor at the same point, nor even with the same intensity; but, for all those involved, something vital had been damaged, something that now seems irreparable.

Obviously, those who lost could not reasonably be expected to overcome such a disaster overnight. They would need time to reflect, to consider, to digest. And it is true that the immediate aftermath of the 1967 war saw an unprecedented intellectual and cultural explosion that lasted for several years, with Beirut as its centre, and contributors from all over the Arab world. Excited and hopeful, I followed its progress, in the newspapers, in discussion groups, at university, and also in the theatres. I particularly remember the controversy surrounding a play written by the Syrian playwright Saadallah Wannous, which dealt sardonically with the recent defeat; its title might be translated as "Soirée for the 5th of June." And I was present when the Syrian poet Omar Abu Risha recited caustic verses about the Arab heads of state who had just met in Morocco to develop a strategy, and had failed to agree.

Fearing shame might dissipate, they stake a claim
And hold a summit in Rabat, to reinforce that shame.

Throughout the Arab world, and particularly in the city where I was born, there was a genuine desire to understand the ills of our societies, and to seek some form of remedy. We were engaged in a form of collective intro-spection. But it did not get very far. Certainly not far enough to trigger a new start. At the time, it was still rare for someone to suggest that religion was the solution, people nurtured other illusions: that the solution came "out of the barrel of a gun," that it was tied to Marxism–Leninism, or a Marxist version of Nasserism ... All these self-proclaimed solutions, whether inspired by Mao, by Che, or by student riots, would lead to disappointment, to tragedy, to confusion. To a series of dead ends.

So much so that, half a century after June 1967, the Arab countries are still "dazed," reeling, unable to come to terms with the trauma of a defeat that still weighs on their chests like a tombstone, and still clouds their minds. They have abandoned pan-Arabism, yet they continue to scorn the existing borders, and hate their leaders. They are no longer waiting for the next war against Israel, but nor do they want peace.

In a much more serious development, they managed to persuade themselves that the rest of the world was in league against them, did not understand them, did not listen to them, did not respect them, that it enjoyed seeing the Arab world humiliated, that there was no point even attempting to change their minds. This, unquestionably, is the most worrying symptom. For those who have been defeated, the worst thing is not defeat itself, but the sense that they will always lose. They end up despising humanity and destroying themselves.

And this is precisely what is happening now in the country of my forefathers.

Why have the Arabs failed to come to terms with their defeat? I can personally attest that many among them constantly ask this question, always anxiously, and often with a hint of self-deprecation to temper their suffering.

For anyone interested in history, this question prompts another: how did other nations react when faced with their most terrible defeats? Down the centuries, every possible scenario has been played out. Earlier, I mentioned the example of France after the defeat of 1940, and the United States after Pearl Harbor; both had suffered serious defeats, but both were able to take their revenge before the war ended. One might also mention the Soviet Union, which, despite being invaded by German troops, was able to recover, to launch a counter-offensive and march into the heart of enemy territory.

This is the perfect scenario for those who have suffered defeat, one that the Arab world attempted to reproduce in October 1973, with the help of Moscow, by launching a surprise attack on the Suez Canal and overrunning the Bar Lev line; but the success was short-lived. Following an airlift to replenish its stock of weapons, Israel was able to retake the advantage. Nasser's successor, Anwar Sadat, learnt his lesson. He agreed to give up the war and sign a peace treaty. Since then, no Arab leader has taken military action against the Jewish state.

Thankfully, however, force is not the only means by which a people can overcome defeat and regain their dignity.

If we consider the countries defeated in the Second World War—notably Germany and Japan, for example—in 1945 they did not pursue rearmament, and in fact attempted to dissociate national pride from military prowess, preferring to focus on industrial and economic development. And, from an economic standpoint, they were extraordinarily successful, and within twenty years were at the forefront of the world's nations, and sometimes the envy of those who had defeated them.

Another example that says much about how a nation can face a major historical ordeal is that of South Korea. Since the mid-twentieth century, the country has been faced with a deeply traumatic situation: the northern half of the peninsula is dominated by a bizarre Communist regime that has developed devastating weapons and is constantly threatening to use them against anyone who crosses its path, including South Korea.

No one would blame South Korea if it had spent the past five decades in a constant state of paranoia; if it still had a repressive military regime and lived in a permanent state of emergency; and if it had devoted its meagre resources to preparing for the looming war. But this is not what South Korea did. After a period of anti-communist dictatorship, it committed itself in the 1980s to becoming a pluralistic, liberal democracy; it has prioritized education, and can now boast one of the most highly educated populations in the world; it has worked to develop its economy and raise the standard of living of its citizens year after year.

When I look at the Republic of Korea today, I can hardly believe that, in the student atlas of my childhood, it was considered part of the "Third World," and ranked behind—often far behind—dozens of countries it has since blithely "overtaken," including Mexico, Argentina, Spain, Turkey, Iran, Iraq, Lebanon, Syria, and even Egypt. The comparison with the latter is particularly instructive. In 1966, per-capita income in South Korea was $130 as compared to $164 in Egypt. Fifty years later, the figure for South Korea was roughly $30,000, as opposed to $2,500 dollars in Egypt. The two countries were no longer "boxing" in the same weight category.

This little country, half of a peninsula, less populous

than Myanmar and smaller than Cuba, is now one of the great industrial powers. Its achievements in technology routinely outstrip those of America, Europe, and Japan; Korean brand names can be found in every home on the planet, on tablets, smartphones, televisions, even robots; South Korea's shipbuilding industry is second only to that of China, while its automobile industry ranks sixth in the world, after China, the USA, Japan, Germany, and India. The same is true in many other industries, where South Korea is surpassed only by countries that are significantly larger and more populous.

The northern half of the peninsula remains separated from the south, and is still ruled by the same bizarre regime which continues to develop weapons and issue threats. South Koreans keep a wary eye on their northern neighbour, but this does not stop them from working, studying, building, moving forward. At times they are forced to walk a tightrope between Washington and Pyongyang, between Washington and Beijing, or between Tokyo and Pyongyang; At times they are forced to meekly endure an affront. But they believe that, one day, their northern compatriots will once again turn to them, at which point they will welcome them, and reintegrate them, as West Germany did East Germany.

It may yet be a long, painful, and sometimes dangerous ordeal, but South Korea has given itself the means to win.

*

As we have seen, there are many different strategies to deal with defeat and with the loss of territory. It is possible to adopt the tried-and-true military strategy that has often given convincing results throughout history; but it is also possible to choose other strategies to overcome the ordeal. The important thing is to think calmly, weigh the pros and cons, choose the most expedient solution, and follow it. And to allow oneself to be guided by intelligence, rather than by anger or the clamour of voices. Above all, it is important to ask the right questions. Not: "Do we have the *right* to use force?" to which the answer is, obviously, "Yes." Nor: "Does our enemy *deserve* to be violently attacked?" to which the answer is also "Yes." But instead: "Is it in *our interest* to adopt a military strategy?" And: "If we resort to force, will the consequences be to our advantage or to the advantage of our enemies?" The answers to these questions require a calm consideration of the balance of power, the available resources, etc.

This approach should be self-evident to anyone involved in politics, and all the more to someone who presides over the fate of a people. Alas, this is not how decisions are made in the Arab world. Even at the most crucial moments. Even by its most devoted and most upstanding leaders.

I have read extensively on the subject of the 1967 war. While the works written by historians and the eyewitness testimonies diverge on a number of aspects of the conflict, all observers—whether Arab, Israeli, Russian, or Western—are agreed on one point: Nasser did not want this war. No doubt he anticipated that, one day, there would be a major conflict between Egypt and the Jewish state. But not at that moment, not in that context, not in that manner. Many of those who spoke to him in the weeks leading up to the war have reported conversations that show Nasser was hesitant, wary; he would rather not have engaged in such a war.

How, then, do we explain why he went ahead? From my readings, I have come to a disconcerting conclusion, one that fits with what was reported at the time: despite his immense popularity, or perhaps because of it, Nasser was vulnerable to demagoguery. Like the tribunes of the ancient world, he longed to hear the crowds cheer him, and he found it difficult to act against them.

In *Parallel Lives* Plutarch cites an uplifting story from Roman history. During battle, when the famous consul Gaius Marius had his troops in an entrenched position, the commander of the enemy forces called to him, "If you are a great general, Marius, come down and fight it out." To which Marius retorted, "If you are a great general, make me fight it out when I do not wish to do so!"

Nasser would have done well to follow his example. He should not have allowed others to choose the date and time of the conflict. Neither his enemies, nor those in the Arab world who were themselves engaged in demagoguery, sometimes out of nationalist fervour, and sometimes in order that they might see him fail.

And so, Nasser stumbled, and when he fell, he brought the Arab world down with him, and for a long time. Speaking of Israel in one of his last speeches, made some months before his death, Nasser said, "Just as the enemy cannot afford to lose a single battle, neither can we afford to lose any more. If the enemy is fighting with his back to the sea, we are fighting with our back to the void."

6

Defeat can be an opportunity; the Arabs failed to seize it. Victory can be a trap; the Israelis failed to avoid it.

In terms of the Arab world, you might think this much is obvious. But in what sense did the war represent a trap for Israel? After all, since 1967, Israel has become the foremost military power in the region; none of its neighbours would dare think to invade it, and so it steps over their borders as it sees fit; it has fashioned such a powerful alliance with the only remaining global superpower that it is impossible to tell who is courting whom; at the same time, it has managed to forge strong links with powers such as Russia, India, and China—formerly the major allies of the Arab world.

I could carry on; the list is long. Since its unexpected victory over Nasser, the status of Israel has changed immeasurably, both regionally and internationally. This has had an impact on the entire Jewish world, which, having suffered thousands of years of humiliation, and survived a holocaust that almost proved fatal, is experiencing unprecedented growth, largely due to the success of the Zionist project—a success no one, not even the most optimistic of its founders, could have foreseen.

At the Paris Peace Conference in Versailles in 1919, among the many people working behind the scenes, were two symbolic figures, one of whom represented the Arab nationalist movement, the other the Jewish nationalist movement. The former was Emir Faisal, son of the Hashemite Sharif of Mecca, future king of the short-lived Arab Kingdom of Syria, and future King of Iraq, accompanied by his esteemed advisor, Lawrence of Arabia; the latter was Chaim Weizmann, a Zionist leader who had been born in the Russian Empire, emigrated to Great Britain, and who, thirty years later, was to become the first President of the State of Israel.

There is a startling photograph that documents an encounter between the two men. In it, Faisal is wearing traditional dress, and Weizmann, standing next to him, is wearing a *keffiyeh* as a sign of brotherhood. There was even a written agreement between the two men, one that praised the "the racial kinship and ancient bonds existing between the Arabs and the Jewish people." While the Emir was prepared to make concessions, he appended a caveat to the agreement: the Arabs would accept the establishment of a Jewish national homeland in Palestine, but only if they were accorded the vast kingdom promised them during the Great War.

Needless to say, none of these things came to pass, and only the most incorrigible dreamers still feel nostalgic for this missed opportunity. I mention it here only as a reminder that these two national movements stood shoulder to shoulder on the international stage, and that their first instinct was to find common ground.

Afterwards, their paths diverged, and their fates, too, dramatically. The Arab nationalist movement, after some remarkable successes, was devastated by a military defeat from which, to my mind, it has never recovered; its heirs are well aware of this fact, and this explains the bitterness, the anguish, and the rage they feel towards themselves and towards the rest of the world.

Should we, conversely, conclude that the Jewish nationalist movement, having succeeded in founding the state to which it aspired, is now thriving and that its heirs are satisfied and content? Anyone who closely follows political and intellectual life in Israel and the Jewish diaspora knows that this is not the case. The movement is plagued by an existential doubt that has proved deep-rooted and tenacious. Although very different to the evil that now plagues the Arab world, nonetheless, in its own way, the situation in Israel is also becoming extremely unsettled.

Rather than examining the countless causes that have been advanced for this existential angst, I shall deal with the dilemma that has crystallized, namely the issue of the occupied territories. What should be done with the West Bank? Israelis have wondered this ever since they seized the land in June 1967. The standard response has been that they would one day withdraw in exchange for a peace agreement. It should be said that there are a number of "secondary issues" about which there has never been consensus: With whom should they make such a peace agreement, and on what terms? Which territories should they withdraw from, and which should they keep? What should be the status of the Palestinian territory? Should it simply be an "autonomous entity" with a police force to maintain law and order; or should it be a fully independent state, with its own army?

Such thorny issues already make the prospect of peace appear remote. And indeed, despite several attempts—some more promising than others, for example the 1993 Oslo Agreement—nothing particularly positive, and certainly nothing conclusive, has happened in recent decades. By the Palestinians, Israeli proposals have been seen—not unreasonably—as the dictates of an occupying force; meanwhile, Israel, being in a position of power and confident that it will remain so, has been in no hurry to make concessions. It could wait for a hundred years, if necessary!

If I have said that the Six-Day War proved disastrous for the victor as well as the vanquished, this is precisely because it favoured a certain mindset among various sections of the Israeli people: What's the hurry? Why should we make concessions? What guarantee do we have that those who sign a peace treaty with us—or their successors—will honour rather than repudiate it? Besides, what can the Arabs do? The military power we once considered fearsome was wiped out in less than a week.

A "peace of the brave" can be agreed only between opponents who respect one another. The sheer brevity of the war of 1967 has undermined that respect and diminished the chances of reaching a fair, freely agreed upon, and sustainable compromise.

Historians and sociologists who have studied Israeli society over recent decades have noted how the image of the Arab and of Arabic culture within this society has been degraded. Perhaps nothing sums up this dismissive attitude better than the fact that a poorly executed job is routinely called "Arab work." There is another symptom: fewer and fewer Israelis consider it worthwhile learning Arabic, even those whose parents spoke it fluently; conversely, young Palestinians are increasingly likely to learn Hebrew and speak it fluently.

I would not go so far as to say that the majority of Israelis had a positive image of Arabs before 1967. That was never the case. Since the late nineteenth century, many of those who settled in Palestine scarcely noticed the local population, and took little interest in what Arabs were doing, what they were thinking, or how they might feel. But, over time, things might have improved, rather than deteriorated. The Jews who fled Iraq, Syria, Lebanon, Morocco, and Yemen might have preserved the linguistic traditions of the countries in which they were born, as they did the musical and culinary traditions. But they have not been encouraged to do so. Neither by their fellow Israeli citizens, nor by the Arabs who were once their compatriots. All in all, there has been little harmony between the Arab and Jewish peoples in recent decades.

The proverbial "alchemy of the Levant" clearly no longer works. Even the sublime complicity of yesteryear has been gradually obliterated. Sometimes I have the impression that I am the only person who still remembers that Maimonides wrote the *Guide for the Perplexed* in Arabic.

*

It is difficult to say for certain whether this burning of cultural bridges played a significant role in reducing the chances of peace. However, there can no doubt that the building of Jewish settlements on the West Bank was a turning point.

In the early days of the occupation, successive Labor Governments in Israel wanted nothing to do with what they called these "informal" settlements. If a peace agreement was one day reached, they reasoned, and it proved necessary to withdraw from the territories, the presence of a large number of Jewish inhabitants would merely complicate the situation, since they would probably have to be relocated against their will.

Their reasoning was sound, but this was a fragile dam that soon began to crack. If one had to put a date on it, the most obvious would be April 20, 1975, when members of the messianic Jewish group known as Gush Emunim seized land from three neighbouring Arab villages and towns to create a Jewish "settlement" called Ofra. The Israeli Army had been issued orders to prevent such settlements, by force, if necessary. Yet, on that day, they hesitated and the militants made the most of it.

Although the Labor Party still held power, conflict had broken out between Prime Minister Yitzhak Rabin and Defence Minister Shimon Peres. The former wanted the settlers evicted; the latter requested that the army not intervene. And so, work on Ofra continued, then another settlement was built, then dozens, then hundreds. A breach had opened in the dam, one that no one has since been able to plug.

Two years after this incident, the Labor Party lost power for the first time since the foundation of the State of Israel. Menachem Begin, former leader of the right-wing nationalist party, became the Head of State, and, unlike his predecessor, he felt no desire to thwart the settlements—which have continued ever since, constantly multiplying, more slowly or more quickly according to circumstances, but in an implacable expansion. As I write this, more than half a million Israelis live on land that, until June 1967, belonged to Arabs.

However one chooses to judge this development, which most Israelis consider legitimate and much of the rest of the world condemns, there can be no doubt that it has created a new reality, one that has radically changed future prospects. The path to peace, already narrow and difficult, is now impassable. In theory, there are various paths Israel could take to address the occupied territories. But, carefully considered, none seem likely to break the deadlock.

One option would be to cede the West Bank to Palestine and repatriate the settlers. This might have been possible when they were merely a handful. Yet that is no longer the case. Any Israeli government that ordered the relocation of hundreds of thousands of Jewish citizens would run the risk of civil war.

A second option, equally theoretical, would be to annex these territories and grant Arab residents citizenship. But that would entail Israel abandoning its fundamental nature as a Jewish state, which is unthinkable; moreover, it would involve Israel competing with the Palestinian people in an area where the latter will surely win: demographics.

A third option would be to annex the land and refuse to grant citizenship to the Arabs, perhaps even encouraging them to leave, as happened during the creation of the State of Israel in 1948. But if Israel were to go down such a path, it would face a bitter, angry condemnation even within the Jewish Diaspora, and further offer ammunition to those who already accuse them of practising a form of apartheid.

There remains the simplest option, one that requires no special measures and no mediation between conflicting views: the status quo. Retain the territories and make no change to their status; indefinitely prolong the occupation without making any declaration that this is a permanent situation; blithely nod every time a new US president offers to mediate a settlement agreement, then wait for him to become disheartened, for his shiny new peace plan to join all the others in the basket.

This is a tried and tested approach. The occupation may be widely criticized around the world, but no one in Israel has an alternative to offer. Although many have tried, no one has yet found a way for an Israeli government, whatever its political affiliation, to solve the problem and break the deadlock. This probably explains why the leaders who favour the "negotiated solution" that long enjoyed widespread support have now been marginalized. Voters feel that, if such leaders were to come to power, they would not know what to do. As a result, the "peace camp," which formerly mobilized huge crowds, has dried to a trickle.

I will always remember what happened in September 1982, in the wake of the Sabra and Shatila massacre near Beirut, in which a Christian-Lebanese militia slaughtered Palestinian civilians within plain sight of Israeli forces. According to some estimates, the death toll was more than two thousand.

The whole world was shocked, the West as much as the Arabs, but the largest and most significant protest took place on the streets of Tel Aviv. The media estimated there were 400,000 demonstrators, that is, one in eight Israeli citizens.

Even those outraged by the behaviour of the authorities and the army could not but admire the attitude of the Jewish people. While protesting wrongs committed against oneself or one's people is legitimate and necessary, it does not automatically indicate a moral elevation; to vociferously protest the wrong done to others by one's own people, on the other hand, shows great dignity and moral conscience. I do not know many people who would have reacted as well.

Sadly, a massive demonstration of this kind would be unthinkable in Israel today. Which, from an ethical standpoint, represents a serious decay.

Although Israel may not be suffering a catastrophic debacle on the scale of that currently suffered by the Arab world, in both cases, we are witnessing a moral and political breakdown that is particularly disturbing. And disheartening. When the heirs to two great civilizations, the custodians of universal dreams, are reduced to a couple of vengeful, vicious tribes, how can one not expect the worst for the future of humanity?

7

It was only many years later, and only from books, that I learnt what really took place on the West Bank on April 20, 1975. At the time, I heard nothing about it. Admittedly, at the time I had more pressing, more traumatic concerns. We had just suffered a tragedy that would tip my native land into an endless war and turn my life and the lives of my family upside down—a horrendous massacre, which my wife and I had the unhappy privilege of seeing with our very eyes.

It happened on a Sunday, April 13. I had just arrived home from a long tour in Asia. At around noon, we heard a commotion in the street. There were people running in all directions, and from close by, behind our building, there were shouts and screams. We went into our bedroom to see what was happening, since it had a large window that overlooked the "mirror junction," so called because a large convex mirror had been installed to allow drivers approaching the junction to see oncoming vehicles that often drove through at full speed. Down in the street was a stationary red-and-white bus and, around it, a group of armed men who had stopped the vehicle. They were arguing with a passenger who was standing at the door of the bus. We were some thirty metres away, too far to hear what was being said, but close enough to catch the tone of the argument and to sense the rising tension.

Suddenly, there was a hail of machine-gun fire. We ducked back behind the bedroom wall. When the shooting subsided a few minutes later, we crept back to the window. The area around the junction was strewn with lifeless bodies. I was not able to see all the victims, since most had been slaughtered before they could get off the bus. Historians of the war in Lebanon usually report that there were twenty-seven fatalities, almost all of them Palestinians. And they agree that "the bus massacre" marked the beginning of the war, even if the foundations had been laid some time earlier.

Having lived through and witnessed the events of the period, I can say that, for me, the massacre was a shock, and in a sense, an enigma, but it was not truly a surprise. All the various players in the looming conflict were already in position, lying in ambush, weapons at the ready; if this had not been the spark, there would have been another.

After the 1967 war, in which my homeland played no role, Lebanon entered a long period of upheaval from which it would never emerge. Given the country's communitarian nature, and the fragility of its institutions, it proved to be the weak link of the Middle East, and for this it paid dearly.

In the wake of the Arab defeat, the recently created Palestinian Liberation Organization, which was looking for a base from which to wage war, attempted to find a foothold in two of Israel's neighbours, Lebanon and Jordan. From a variety of standpoints, Jordan seemed like the ideal solution. Half of its population was Palestinian, it shared a long border with the Jewish state, and was adjacent to the West Bank, all of which facilitated incursions and contacts with militants in the occupied territories.

But "little King" Hussein of Jordan was obstinate and hardheaded. He was prepared to give some latitude to the Palestinian movement, but not enough for it to become a state within a state. By turns firm and conciliatory, alternating strong-arm tactics and ceasefires, he gradually managed to tilt the balance of power in his favour.

Then in September 1970—a time which some, as a sign of mourning, call "Black September"—he launched a major military offensive to regain control of the territory. The fedayeen, inadequately equipped and no match for an army loyal to its king, were forced to retreat. Their leader, Yasser Arafat, who had just stepped onto the international stage and whose popularity kept growing, requested that President Nasser personally intervene to deal with the mess. An extraordinary summit of Arab heads of state was held in Cairo. Negotiations went on through the night, amid promises, threats, slammed doors, and insincere handshakes.

On the last day of this gruelling conference, while tirelessly shuttling his guests from his residence to the airport, the Egyptian president collapsed and died of a heart attack.

Hours earlier, he had persuaded his peers to adopt an agreement putting an end to the fighting, one that, in vague terms, acknowledged the Palestinians' right to continue their struggle against Israel by any means. But this had merely been a face-saving exercise. In practical terms, King Hussein had won a decisive victory and his country would never again serve as a base for armed resistance.

*

The fedayeen in Lebanon were to experience a very different fate.

Initially, they assumed the country would simply be an additional base, allowing them to generate media coverage of their actions, but not a theatre for those actions. It did not share a border with the West Bank, and, in Lebanon, Palestinian refugees represented only a small fraction of the population.

In addition, the complexity of politics in Lebanon was legendary. How could they deal with so many religions, factions, clans, and hereditary chiefs? But, very quickly, Arafat and his companions began to understand that, far from being an obstacle to their ambitions, this complexity offered boundless opportunities, if they could manoeuvre intelligently.

When people talk about the unfathomable intricacies of Lebanese politics, they sometimes fail to mention the fact that the Maronite Christian community, from which every president is drawn, also has a monopoly on another key post: commander in chief of the army. I have already mentioned General Chehab, who assumed the presidency during the 1958 crisis, since which time the two roles had become so closely associated that it became a custom to only elect generals to the presidency.

This curious custom may well prove temporary. Nonetheless, rightly or wrongly, the army has long been perceived as a Maronite stronghold, and this perception played a decisive role during the crucial period when the Palestinian movements sought to create a base in Lebanon. At the time, many Muslims were deeply mistrustful of the Lebanese Army, which they criticised for not fighting alongside other Arab armies. "Maybe they wanted our country to be invaded and occupied, too?" sneered one politician of the time. Nonetheless, it is certainly true that, amid the bitterness and anger that followed defeat, Lebanon's failure to participate in the war against Israel was considered by some, if not treason, at the very least an indifference to the Arab cause.

As a result, when armed fedayeen first appeared on the streets of Beirut and other parts of the country proclaiming their intention to wage war on the enemy, a certain section of the populace identified with them and offered them help. The Lebanese authorities could do little but accept this fate. Not because they approved of the fedayeen, or because they underestimated the risks that their presence in the country might entail, but because they felt unable to prevent it.

In a communitarian system, when there is no consensus, political power becomes paralysed. And on the subject of the fedayeen, there was no consensus—even within the army. Although the Maronites were probably slightly better represented in the key army positions, as a whole, the army reflected Lebanese society and suffered from the same ethnic and ideological fault lines. If it were to engage in such a contentious battle, it might well fall apart.

It was because of this crippling weakness that, after a handful of early skirmishes with the fedayeen, the Lebanese government hastily accepted what the Hashemite King of Jordan would reject until the bitter end: a duly signed treaty allowing Palestinian armed movements to operate within its territory. Signed in Cairo in November 1969 and blindly ratified by a Lebanese parliament whose members were not allowed to read its secret clauses, the agreement will be remembered as the epitome of what a state must avoid if it wishes to preserve its sovereignty and its civil peace. According to the agreements, the Palestinian refugee camps in Lebanon were now under the jurisdiction of the Palestinian Liberation Organization, which was now free to conduct military actions against Israel from Lebanese soil.

It is absolutely legitimate for a government to take part in a war it considers just, or to offer assistance to those waging that war. But when a small, fragile country that has little in common with Prussia or Sparta is thrust into a war without being allowed to decide whether or not to join the conflict, merely because it is a useful scapegoat for other countries or political organizations, it is neither legitimate nor acceptable.

This is precisely what happened in my native country; it was violently pushed to the brink of a volcano. Neither did it have the consolation of being seen as an innocent victim, since throughout this ordeal there were local factions, Left and Right, Christian and Muslim, prepared to give the predators a leg-up.

This is the price my compatriots and I were forced to pay for failing to build a nation.

The Cairo Agreement had already come into force by the time the Palestinian organizations were expelled from Jordan. As a result, they could fall back on Beirut, which, for a dozen years, became their de facto capital, as well as the capital of the Lebanese state. It was here that leaders, including Arafat, chose to live. It was here that foreign delegations met with them. It was her that their governing bodies met. And it was from here that they issued their military communiqués and their political statements.

The city quickly became become a home from home for the international press and intelligence services from around the world. It was crawling with double agents, fake diplomats, activists, and adventurers; they infiltrated the Palestinian organizations, spied on them, preyed on them, or lived within their sphere of influence. How often did I later hear that some particular militant faction, whether from West or East, had cut its teeth in the Lebanon of that period? We had not yet reached the era of Islamist-inspired suicide bombings, but this was the era of spectacular aeroplane hijackings, violent far-left splinter groups like the Japanese Red Army, the Baader–Meinhof Group, and the shadowy organization that called itself "Black September."

To say that opening itself up to factions of every hue and stripe meant my native country was courting trouble would be an understatement. There ensued a long series of violent reprisals by the Israelis that culminated in a massive invasion of the country, as far as Beirut; meanwhile there were constant encroachments by Arab nations that fractured the country, bled it dry, and meant that, for three decades, it was effectively under the thumb of Damascus. To say nothing of the endless wars involving a variety of forces, all of which were destructive and deadly. There were hundreds of thousands of victims, the country's economy was all but wiped out, while development and modernization were deferred for a long time.

I have painted a somewhat apocalyptic picture of Lebanon during these years, one I feel I should qualify. Because the Lebanon of the time was not merely a succession of militia training camps and spy networks. In the wake of the fedayeen came researchers, writers, publishers, filmmakers, playwrights, singers—many Palestinian, but also Syrian, Iraqi, Sudanese, and North African—all of whom contributed to the cultural explosion that flourished in the wake of the 1967 debacle.

Because of their presence, and the psychological and emotional tensions this generated, Beirut's role as the intellectual and artistic capital of the Arab world would experience an extraordinary flowering.

8

As chance would have it, I began my career as a journalist in the first months of 1971, just as the Palestinian Liberation Organization (PLO) was establishing a presence in Beirut, and thereby thrusting it into the media spotlight for years to come. I was twenty-two, I was working for *An-Nahar*, one of the country's leading newspapers, and, as a result, I had an unparalleled observation post.

The newspaper's editorial was a constant parade of characters I would never have had the opportunity to meet had I lived in a different city, or at a different time. I would occasionally encounter the German (or Algerian, or Soviet) Ambassador when taking the lift, a Greek Orthodox bishop, a leader of the Eritrean independence movement, or a former Lebanese army colonel who had been pardoned and released after being sentenced to death for an attempted military coup. Stepping into the cramped office I shared with three other journalists, I often found my colleagues having a clandestine meeting with a reporter from the *Guardian* or *Le Monde*, or a special correspondent from *Der Spiegel* or *Newsweek*, who had come to find out what was happening or to confirm some rumour they had heard.

Among the regular visitors to the editorial department was the official spokesman for the PLO, Kamal Nasser. Born in the West Bank to a Protestant family, Nasser was a journalist and poet in his own right, a former member of the Jordanian Parliament. He had been tasked by Arafat with raising the Palestinian Liberation Organization's profile in the international press, and proved himself to be very efficient in doing so. Within a very short time, he succeeded in giving the Palestinian movement a humane and engaging face, and an eloquent voice that had nothing in common with diehard propagandists. He would digress from sanctimonious waffle to chat about his days as a student at the American University of Beirut, or recite one of his own poems about the bistros of Paris. I even heard him enthusiastically praise the chivalrous nature of King Hussein, despite the fact that, at the time, Hussein was the sworn enemy of the Palestinians. "He slaughtered us, but I can't bring myself to hate him!" he said, spreading his hands in a gesture of helplessness. Foreign correspondents liked him, especially since his English was exceptionally fluent. In fact, early in his career, he had taught English at a missionary school in Jerusalem.

I took great interest and no little pleasure in listening to him, even when he was sticking strictly to his role as official PLO spokesperson. But I never took notes, and I had no intention of using his comments. As a journalist, I was not responsible for Palestinian affairs, or Lebanese affairs, or anything related to the Arab world. *An-Nahar* had a large and competent team to deal with such issues. Specialists were assigned to cover every major country; they diligently followed the news, regularly visited the country, and were intimately acquainted with the leadership, the opposition, and numerous reliable sources.

The subject to which I devoted my time was simultaneously vast and peripheral. Vast since, in theory, it spanned the whole planet outside the Arab world; peripheral to the extent that readers are primarily interested in local news—news that might affect their lives and those of their families. Needless to say, any newspaper conscious of its prestige had to cover the Vietnam War, the struggle against apartheid in South Africa, the Carnation Revolution in Portugal, the coup d'état in

Chile, or the military uprising against Emperor Haile Selassie in Ethiopia. As a result, *An-Nahar* encouraged my passion for far-off lands, and sometimes encouraged me to visit so I could get to know them more closely. But the vast world usually took up a very modest number of pages.

Since I was not tasked with covering the events going on around me, I adapted to the role of mute observer with little trouble. However, on a number of occasions, the pressures of reporting were such that all hands were needed, including mine.

Such an emergency occurred on the night of April 9, 1973. I was coming home from a party with friends when I heard on the radio that there had been a serious incident. The bulletin was confused and fragmented. It appeared that Israel had launched a raid on certain sectors of the city, but there was no information about the targets. I went straight to the newspaper office, where the editorial department was in chaos. It was not until 3 a.m. that we began to receive more precise information. Special units from the Israeli Defence Forces had landed on the coast near Beirut, and commando teams had been dispatched to launch attacks on various targets in at least three sectors of the city before returning to their boats and withdrawing.

Some minutes later, on national radio, we learnt that there had been an attack on a group of buildings where a number of Palestinian leaders lived in the western part of the capital, near rue Verdun. Two of the leaders had been killed, and a third, Kamal Nasser, had been abducted.

Sam Mazmanian, the star photographer for *An-Nahar*, who also contributed to two major US news agencies,

Associated Press and United Press, immediately decided to visit the scene. I was asked to go with him.

A crowd had gathered outside the buildings—armed fedayeen, neighbours in pyjamas, onlookers. One man told me to be careful, since there were unexploded detonators still lying around on the ground. Another lent me a flashlight, because the electricity had been cut off and the stairwell was in darkness. Still another told me that the PLO spokesman lived on the third floor.

The door to the apartment was wide open, there was debris everywhere. Warily, I stepped inside, and was quickly joined by Sam, who had stopped to take pictures in the stairwell. The place looked deserted. But suddenly, I saw a body under the dining table. Whoever had been here before us had obviously not seen it. I turned the beam of the flashlight. It was him. Kamal Nasser. Lying on his back, his arms spread wide. There was a bullet wound beneath his lower lip. It was too dark for me to see whether there were any others.

I was standing, upset and lost in thought, when my colleague laid a hand on my shoulder. He wanted me to move aside so that he could take a picture.

Back at the newspaper offices, I hurriedly corrected the information that had been circulating. "He was not abducted; he was killed. I found his body lying under his table in the dark. Sam has the pictures; he's developing them right now."

Years later, we would learn that the April 1973 operation had been led by Ehud Barak, future Prime Minister of Israel, dressed as a woman and wearing a dark wig. The disguise was part of a ruse to simulate a love scene in a car, so that when the guards in the street came over to investigate, they could be silently liquidated before the commandos stormed the building.

Two months earlier, a thirty-seven-year-old American novelist had rented an apartment in the same group of buildings. She was working on a book based on the life of Lady Hester Stanhope, an English adventurer well known in the Levant, where she had lived for many years in the early nineteenth century. The young novelist's extensive research was piled on a desk by the window; from here she could see the desk in the opposite apartment where Kamal Nasser sat down to write. Not until forty years later did she reveal her true identity—and even then, she did not give her real name—in a book called *Yael – the Mossad's Warrior in Beirut*. She explains that, in order to make her cover story more convincing, her superiors had sent her to spend a few days with a genuine historian, Shabtai Teveth, the author of a biography of Moshe Dayan and several books on David Ben-Gurion; not so that he could teach her to write, something she did not feel able to do, she says, but so that he could teach her to *pretend*: how to convincingly leave documents on her desk, where to keep her pens, what to throw into the wastepaper basket, and how to talk to other people about her literary work. A panoply of minutely detailed preparations with a simple goal: to keep watch on the Palestinian leadership and ensure they would be home when the Israeli commandos came to assassinate them.

That evening, April 9, a Mossad officer, someone posing as a tourist passing through Beirut, invited "Yael" for a drink in the bar of one of the big hotels.

"Are your neighbours home?" he asked.

"Yes, all three of them."

Had she given a different answer, the man would have called his contact to postpone the attack.

*

Given the prominence of the Palestinian victims, and the fantastical nature of the Israeli operation, Lebanon was shaken as it had seldom been before. It triggered a grave governmental crisis. The prime minister, Saeb Salam, demanded the immediate dismissal of the commander of the army and, when his demand was rejected by President Suleiman Frangieh, he tendered his resignation.

This was a typically Lebanese piece of communitarian gamesmanship, given that Salam was a Sunni Muslim while Frangieh was a Maronite Christian, as was the general who was threatened with dismissal. But there was also a genuine dilemma that went beyond such political divisions, one that worried all those interested in the fate of the country.

Obviously, it does not look good for a national army expected to defend the territory of the country when enemy commandos arrive under cover of darkness, attack targets in three or four different districts of the capital, and manage to escape without being intercepted. The whole country felt humiliated, and was furious with the army. Could they not have fired a few shots, for the sake of it? Probably. But there was another aspect to the problem, one that could not be ignored: the Cairo Agreement had limited the powers of the Lebanese Army in allowing Palestinians to launch military operations from the territory it was supposed to protect. Could the Lebanese Army be made to shoulder responsibility for the military reprisals when it was explicitly forbidden from preventing the attacks that incited those reprisals? These are two complementary, inextricable responsibilities that face armies all over the world; if they are stripped of one, how can they be asked to fulfil the other?

Beyond the arguments about the duties and responsibilities of the Lebanese Army, it was now abundantly clear that there was no way for the state of Lebanon to extricate itself from a deadlock that had turned the country into both a combat zone and a collateral victim of the bloody clashes between the Israelis and the Palestinians.

Around the country, many communities began to create militias, to build up arsenals. Meanwhile new leaders suddenly appeared to be arguing about something hitherto unthinkable: since the army was clearly unable to fulfil its mission, the "citizens" would do so themselves. But not all of these so-called "citizens" shared the same vision. For some, the army's duty was to oppose Israel, regardless of the cost. For others, it was to oppose the Palestinians.

The former were mostly to be found in the Muslim communities and left-wing parties, which, for a time, earned them the absurd title "Islamic progressives"; they pledged to protect the Palestinian resistance against all those who sought to stifle or hinder it; in return, the PLO rewarded them with weapons, money, and military training.

The latter was spearheaded by parties from within the Christian communities; they saw the Palestinian military presence as a threat to the country and hoped to end it. They provided intensive weapons training for militants, though they knew that they were outnumbered and needed a powerful ally.

To whom could they turn in search of an ally? Some thought of Israel. But, at the time, the idea commanded little support. It would later be briefly explored by Bachir Gemayel, and it would end on a double tragedy: the assassination of the young president-elect, followed by the Sabra and Shatila massacre.

At the time, another option prevailed, one that would bring its share of tragedy. Although advocated by President Frangieh, it found little enthusiasm among other Maronite leaders, though most considered it the lesser of two evils: rather than turning to Israel, and ending up as the pariah of the Arab world, might it not be better to allow a "sister country"—namely Syria—to "tame" the fedayeen?

Everyone knew that Arafat and President Hafez al-Assad despised each other. This was not a mere clash of personalities, but a major dispute over strategies.

Throughout the struggle, the PLO leader's constant concern was that the Palestinians' "decision" should remain in their hands, and that no Arab leader was entitled to speak in their name. Assad, on the other hand, argued that the Palestinian cause concerned the whole Arab nation, "from the ocean to the Gulf." A statement of principle that bolstered one of the Syrian president's key strategic goals: the ability to play the "Palestinian card," which, in negotiations with the major powers in this conflict, represented a major asset.

In support of this objective, Damascus had established a network of pro-Syrian organizations within the PLO, and at the very heart of Fatah, the movement founded by Arafat, to promote Assad's ideas. If Assad could gain control over Lebanon, if he could be seen as an arbitrator in the country, a patron to both the Palestinians and the Lebanese, protecting each against the other, he would be in a strong position in any Middle Eastern negotiations.

When Lebanese leaders went to Damascus to ask for help in extricating themselves from the quicksand in which they were foundering, their words were music to Assad's ears. It was too good an opportunity to miss, and he grasped it with both hands. And so, Syrian troops poured into the country, and when Arafat and his "Islamic progressives" attempted to stand up to them, they were roundly defeated.

In the Christian area where I was living, many people applauded the Syrian Army, who had finally "liberated" the Palestinian militias. Others were already asking who the hell was going to eventually "liberate" the Syrian Army.

*

The day I left war-torn Lebanon on a rickety boat, in June 1976, all the dreams of the Levant in which I had been born were dead or dying. The paradise my mother had known had been razed to the ground, while that of my father was a shadow of its former self. The Arabs were trapped by their defeats, the Israelis by their victories, and neither could wrest themselves free.

Needless to say, I could not know how contagious the tragedies of my native land would prove, nor how brutally its moral and political decline would spread across the globe. But I was not entirely surprised by what happened. Having been born on the fault line, I did not need some exceptional gift of foresight to realize that we were fast approaching the abyss.

I had only to keep my eyes open, and listen for the rending sound of the quake.

III

The Year of the Great Reversal

As the future ripens in the past,
so the past rots in the future—
a terrible festival of dead leaves.

Anna Akhmatova (1889–1966)
"Poem without a Hero"

1

The tragedy that Arabs today simply call "Sixty-Seven" was thus a watershed on the road to despair and destruction—but it does not explain everything. Things might have worked out; the Arab world might have taken a different turning some years later and got back on its feet. The fact that this drift has not merely continued but worsened is the result of a wide-ranging historical phenomenon that has occurred over a long period of time and cannot, strictly speaking, be considered a single "event."

In fact, the word that comes to my mind is *syndrome*, in the original, the earliest sense of the word: "a place where several roads run in the same direction." As a result, what I will try to evoke in the pages that follow is a vast number of events, spanning many continents and various domains, all of which share a common direction, and which have somehow dragged the people "yoked" to them down the path on which they now find themselves.

In trying to understand why a given situation develops in a particular way, it is often tempting to look to the distant past. This can become a long and tedious process, since each individual aspect has its own history, which may stretch back centuries. To avoid getting lost in the dense jungle of dates, characters, passions, and myths, it is sometimes necessary to take a machete and clear a path forwards to gain some perspective.

This is what I did when I plunged into the history of recent decades. Perhaps I should say "re-plunged," because, since my youth, I have closely followed the news, with a mania that can be explained by the fact that I grew up in the shadow of my journalist father.

It is a passion that has never wavered. Even now, I spend several hours every day reading and listening to news from all parts of the world. And even when I find events worrying or distressing, I never tire of the spectacle, I never turn away. I constantly feel as though I am watching an extraordinary soap opera with an infinite number of exciting episodes, and twists worthy of the finest screenwriters.

Most of what I am about to discuss entails events I was aware of when they occurred; sometimes, I travelled there—to Saigon, Tehran, New Delhi, Aden, Prague, New York, and Addis Ababa—and witnessed them in person. However, events seem different in hindsight, when we know their consequences. What became clear to me when I revisited "yesterday's news" was that a series of decisive events occurred around 1979 whose importance I did not fully understand at the time. Events that triggered a kind of "reversal" of ideas and attitudes throughout the world that has proved enduring. The fact that they occurred so close together was not the result of concerted action; nor was it mere coincidence. I would call it a "synchronicity." It was as though a new "season" was dawning, and its flowers blossomed in a thousand places at once. Or as though the "spirit of the age" was heralding the end of one cycle and the beginning of another.

This notion, which German philosophy calls the *zeitgeist*, is less ghostly than it might appear; in fact, it is crucial to understanding the march of history. People who are contemporaries influence each other in various ways, usually unbeknownst to them. We emulate each other, even mimic each other, we conform to prevailing attitudes, sometimes merely out of protest. And we do so in every domain—in art, literature, philosophy, politics, and medicine, just as much as in our clothes, our appearance, or our hairstyles.

The means by which this *geist*, this "ghost," spreads and dominates are difficult to identify; but it is indisputable that it has done so, in every era, with ruthless efficiency. And in the age of instantaneous mass communication such influences spread much more rapidly than before.

Usually, the influence of the zeitgeist goes unnoticed. But sometimes, the effects are so blatant that they can almost be seen in real time. This is certainly the impression I had while poring over recent history in an attempt to draw lessons from it.

How could I not have noticed the powerful correlation between events? I should long ago have come to the conclusion that now seems to me self-evident: that we had embarked on an eminently paradoxical era in which our worldview was to be transformed, and even inverted. Suddenly *it was conservatism that styled itself as revolutionary, while the left wing and the advocates of "progressivism" had no other purpose than to preserve the status quo.*

In my notes, I started to write about a "year of reversal," or sometimes a "year of great sea change," and to enumerate the remarkable events that seemed to justify these names. They are many and, in these pages, I will mention some of them. But two in particular seemed acutely symbolic: the Islamic revolution proclaimed by Ayatollah Khomeini in Iran in February 1979; and the conservative revolution in the United Kingdom, spearheaded by Prime Minister Margaret Thatcher beginning in May 1979.

A vast ocean separates these two events, and these two notions of conservatism. And also, of course, the two key characters; to find an equivalent of what happened in Iran with Khomeini would entail going back to the time of Cromwell, when the regicidal revolutionaries were messianic Puritans. Nonetheless, there are similarities between these two upheavals beyond the coincidence of dates. In both cases, we see the revolutionary standard being raised in the name of social forces and ideologies that, until then, had been the victims, or at least the targets, of modern revolutions: in one case, the defenders of moral and religious order; in the other, the proponents of economic and social order.

Both of these revolutions were to have major global repercussions. With the election of Ronald Reagan to the presidency, Mrs. Thatcher's ideas would quickly spread to the United States; meanwhile Khomeini's vision of a revolutionary, traditionalist Islam, one resolutely inimical to the West, spread throughout the world, taking on many forms, and driving out more conciliatory approaches.

I will address these differences and similarities, but first I would like to briefly digress to counter any simplistic view that such a comparison might elicit.

In attempting to understand how the political and mental landscape around the world has been "turned on its head" in recent decades, it is important to avoid thinking of the conservative revolution in the West as merely "usurping" the concept of revolution, because, in many crucial aspects, and in its consequences, it was genuinely revolutionary; in particular, it played an instrumental role in the technological advances then taking place, which marked a significant change in human history; and it was decisive in the economic rise of China, India, and many other countries, which is also a major global development.

If what is initially striking about Khomeini's revolution in Iran is its dogged traditionalism, particularly in matters of clothing, this should not blind us to the corrosive radicalism that the Iranian example has fostered throughout the Muslim world, which has shaken every power in the region.

Since the sixteenth century, the concept of "revolution"—appropriated by political factions from the movement of celestial bodies—has been applied to many very different events, so, rather than question whether one can legitimately apply the word to the events in Tehran and London in 1979, we should attempt to understand the reasons for the upheaval experienced around the world in that year, and which have changed the meaning and the gist of the word's usage.

Having made these clarifications, I would like to return to the conservative revolutions I previously mentioned.

The rise of Margaret Thatcher would not have had the same impact had it not been part of a broader, deeper movement that would quickly spread beyond the borders of Britain. First to the United States, with the election of Ronald Reagan in November 1980, and then to the rest of the world. The guiding principles of the Anglo-American conservative revolution would be embraced by leaders from right and left, sometimes enthusiastically, sometimes resignedly. The notions of reducing government intervention in the economy, cutting social spending, giving entrepreneurs greater freedom, and quashing the influence of trade unions would quickly come to be seen as the benchmarks of good governance.

One of the key books of the conservative revolution was *Atlas Shrugged*, a novel by Ayn Rand, a Russian emigrant who settled in the United States. The story revolves around a strike organized, not by labourers, but by entrepreneurs and "creative minds" frustrated by excessive regulation. The title conjures the image of the mythological Atlas who, weary of carrying the world on his shoulders, shrugs it off—the verb evokes frustration and defiance.

This philosophical novel, first published in 1957, which became the bible of American conservatives who favoured a form of resolutely anti-statist "libertarianism," has since been overtaken by reality. The uprising by the rich against the encroachments of a state determined to redistribute wealth may not have happened as Rand suggested, but it has happened nonetheless. And it has been hugely successful. The result has been a stark increase in social inequality, to the point of creating a small caste of multi-billionaires, each of whom has more wealth than many nations.

The second "conservative revolution," the one which took place in Iran, was also to have significant repercussions throughout the world.

This revolution was not a revolution by the rich against the poor—quite the contrary, it was waged in the name of the poor, the "wretched of the earth," and in this sense it followed on from numerous other revolutions in the twentieth century. What was atypical was that it was led by a socially conservative clergy, frustrated by reforms that, they felt, ran counter to religious and traditional values.

2

To these two revolutions, which took place within the space of three months and which neatly encapsulate the atypical upheavals of our age, I would add two other events, which are no less significant, and which offer a more complete picture.

In December 1978, at the Third Plenum of the 11th Central Committee Congress of the Communist Party of China, Deng took over the reins of power and launched his own "conservative revolution." Deng never used this phrase, and it was certainly a very different revolution to those seen in Tehran and London, but it was part of the same zeitgeist. It was conservative in inspiration, since it was a return to the ancient merchant traditions of the Chinese people that Mao Zedong's revolution had attempted to root out. It was also revolutionary because, in the space of a single generation, it would radically transform life in the largest nation on the planet; in the course of history, few revolutions have so profoundly changed the lives of so many men and women in such a short space of time.

The other notable event took place in Rome, in October 1978, when Pope John Paul II became head of the Catholic Church.

Born in Poland, Karol Wojtyła combined social and doctrinal conservatism with the fighting spirit of a revolutionary leader. "Be not afraid!" he said in his first address to the faithful gathered in St. Peter's Square on the day of his enthronement. "Open wide the doors for Christ. To his saving power open the boundaries of States, economic and political systems, the vast fields of culture, civilization, and development." His influence was to prove critical.

Did these four major upheavals, which took place in the seven months between October 1978 and May 1979, in radically different social and cultural settings, have anything in common beyond the mere "coincidence" of their timing? Is it possible that the Roman Curia, the Central Committee of the Communist Party of China, the British electorate, and the Iranian protesters were responding to a similar impulse?

In hindsight, there are two main factors that, to my mind, weighed heavily on the period, which affected every country of the world to varying degrees, and which may have played a role in spurring the four events I have just mentioned. The first is the terminal decline of the Soviet regime; the second is the oil crisis.

The latter I will discuss in greater detail in subsequent chapters; for the moment, let me just say that the oil crisis forced every country on earth to question the management of its economy, its social legislation, and its ties with the oil-exporting countries; meanwhile, for those in the Arab-Muslim world, this "crisis," which should have ensured their happiness, was to prove devastating and ultimately catastrophic.

As for the decline of the Soviet regime, in hindsight it now seems to me that many of the events of this period were reactions—more or less direct, more or less conscious, more or less considered—to the actions of the "sick man" that the Soviet regime had become. A deeply strange "sick man" that still considered itself healthy and powerful and believed it had its enemies on the ropes.

*

Looking back on the 1970s, it is difficult not to find it pathetic, this spectacle of a superpower throwing itself into a strategy of conquest on multiple continents, while the foundations of its own house, with its tattered banners of socialism, progressivism, militant atheism, and egalitarianism, were irreparably fractured and about to collapse.

To anyone who trusted to superficial appearances, the Soviet Union seemed to be going from strength to strength. The Vietnam War, a titanic clash between communism and capitalism waged since the end of World War II, finally came to an end in April 1975. South Vietnam, which, since 1955, had been a republic supported by the United States, was conquered by the Northern forces with the support of the local communist movement, which called itself the National Liberation Front for South Vietnam, or simply the Viet Cong.

As a young journalist, fascinated as were so many others by this war, symbolic to my generation, I had gone to Saigon to witness the decisive battle. I knew that the war was in its end stage, but never imagined how swiftly events would develop. When I arrived on March 26, the former imperial capital of Hue was captured by Communist forces; a week later, they were seven hundred kilometres further south, on the outskirts of Saigon—and it was clear that nothing would halt their progress.

In the capital of South Vietnam, there seemed little will to fight. I sensed only resignation, and even panic. Those who feared the harshness of the coming regime were desperately seeking some way of fleeing the country. Overnight, the South Vietnamese dong lost all value; no one was prepared to accept the currency. In government offices, people hastily took down the official photographs of General Thieu, the last president of South Vietnam, who fled the country and peacefully ended his days in Massachusetts, forgotten by everyone.

The fall of Saigon occurred on April 30. Those who lived through those times will never forget the pitiful scenes of civilians and soldiers who had sought refuge in the US embassy, clinging desperately to the last helicopters in an attempt to escape. Images that were all the more humiliating for the saviours than for the survivors. The "Republic of Vietnam," which a succession of American presidents had vowed to defend, was annexed by the Socialist Republic of Vietnam and its capital renamed Ho Chi Minh City, after the general who had successfully routed France and then the United States.

Two weeks earlier in Cambodia, Phnom Penh had been seized by Communist insurgents; then came the turn of Laos. The famous "domino effect," which predicted that if one country came under the influence of Communism, the surrounding countries would follow, seemed to be playing out. And the principal beneficiary was the Soviet Union.

Nor was this phenomenon limited to Southeast Asia. In Africa, for example, where the former European colonial powers still held a prominent role, the balance of power was rapidly shifting. In the wake of the Carnation Revolution of April 1974, when Portugal granted independence to its colonies, the five new African countries were all governed by Marxist parties; the richest of them, Angola, even called on Fidel Castro to intervene to stem an uprising, leading Cuba to launch a large-scale intervention with Soviet support, landing tens of thousands of troops on the Angolan coast in November 1975 without any opposition from the United States.

And so, in the months that followed their highly symbolic victory in the Vietnam War, the Soviets had made spectacular progress on a continent that had previously been the preserve of the West. The number of sub-Saharan countries with Marxist governments quickly swelled—in addition to Angola, Mozambique, Cape Verde, Guinea-Bissau, and São Tomé and Príncipe, there were Madagascar, the Republic of the Congo, and Guinea ... For a brief period, Ethiopia and Somalia, the two major countries in the Horn of Africa, were ruled by Marxist–Leninist military regimes, while on the far shore of the Gulf of Aden, the independent state of South Yemen declared a "people's democratic republic" complete with communist party and politburo.

It was amid this unfettered expansion and sheer euphoria that the Soviet leaders embarked on a venture that would prove disastrous, indeed fatal to the Soviet regime: the Afghanistan War.

There were already a number of active and ambitious Communist militias in the mountainous country bordered by Iran, Pakistan, China, and the Soviet republics of Central Asia; nonetheless a small minority of the socially conservative Muslim population was fiercely hostile to foreign interference. Left to themselves, the militia could not secure and retain power. Only an intervention by their powerful Soviet neighbours could swing the balance of power in their favour. But first they had to convince their neighbours of the need for such an intervention.

This is precisely what happened in April 1978. Infuriated by the increasing rapprochement between Kabul and the West, anxious to preserve their border security and the stability of their republics, and convinced they could act with impunity, Soviet leaders backed a coup d'état by Marxist factions. When the new regime was met with a popular uprising, the Soviet Union sent in troops to crush the unrest, and every day sank a little deeper into the mire.

As so often throughout history—though each time people believe things will turn out differently—the Soviet leaders were convinced that their "pacifying mission" would be brief, and result in a decisive victory.

This deeply reckless strategy can be explained only by the leaders' assessment of their enemies' attitudes at the time. They believed that the United States, traumatized by the long and disastrous war in Vietnam, would have no desire to engage in some new conflict overseas, and so, if Soviet troops began a war with Afghanistan, they would meet no opposition from the Americans. After all, surely their failure to respond when Cuban troops had marched into Angola demonstrated that the United States no longer had an appetite for armed conflict?

As they surveyed the world around them, the Soviet leaders assumed that they had nothing to fear. Not from the United States, nor from Western Europe, which was still struggling with the consequences of the oil crisis; and not from China, where the death of Mao Zedong in September 1976 had led to what looked to be a long war of succession.

The Soviets were not mistaken in assuming that no one would get in their way, and they marched on Kabul.

3

But Moscow had underestimated its opponents' ability to regroup, and indeed to counterattack, in various domains, and various theatres of operation.

This most notably occurred in Britain. On the eve of the May 1979 general election, which would sweep the Iron Lady to power, the country was in a wretched state. Strikes, riots, blackouts, a toxic social atmosphere, and the feeling among Labour leaders—and indeed among many moderate conservatives—was that these were simply the repercussions of the oil crisis, and that there was no choice but to "muddle through" and wait for things to improve. The image that came to define this period was one of Piccadilly Circus plunged into darkness because of the miners' strikes. The British historian Andy Beckett offers an account of these dark times in a book called *When the Lights Went Out.*

Mrs. Thatcher had burst onto the national stage with a very different mindset and approach. Decline is not inevitable, she told her fellow citizens, we can and we must reverse it; we must set a course and not continue wavering, we must ruthlessly crush all those who would stand in our way—beginning with the trade unions. In the year Thatcher came to power, almost three million working days were lost due to industrial action.

The country had no choice but to sink or to bounce back. As it had done at other times in its troubled history, Britain chose to listen to the stubborn voice that promised to lead it out of the impasse, head held high, even if it meant painful sacrifices.

From this jump start, the conservative revolution was born. One of its effects was to end the embarrassment that the right wing had felt in political and intellectual debates, particularly on social issues. This is a difficult notion to grasp, and one that is impossible to quantify, but it is essential to understanding the sea change that has occurred in attitudes around the world.

When faced with a prevailing opinion, those who do not share it must use cunning and tact, they may even pretend to accept some of its principles so that their objections can be heard. In many European countries, the intellectual and moral "high ground" had long been dominated by the ideas and the vocabulary of the left. The example that immediately springs to mind is that of my adopted country, France. I have lived here for over forty years, and I have had the opportunity to observe and to listen to its politicians, its intellectuals, its academics.

Until the 1980s, few leaders openly claimed to be right-wing; those not on the left preferred to call themselves centrists, and when they criticized communists, they felt obliged to preface their criticisms by saying that they were not "anti-communist," which was considered a derogatory term at the time. Today, precisely the reverse is true: those on the right proudly proclaim their affiliation; while anyone inclined to express a positive opinion about any aspect of communism feels compelled to preface it by insisting that they in no way subscribe to this ideology. I made use of this verbal equivocation only a few pages ago ...

To get back to Britain, one might say that before the Thatcherite revolution no political leader, whether left- or right-wing, wanted to be seen as a scab, as an enemy of the unions, as insensitive to the fate of miners and other low-income workers; nor did they want be seen as responsible for the death of a prisoner on hunger strike, like Bobby Sands in 1981. The Iron Lady's morally questionable but historically incontestable contribution is that she blithely committed all the "sins" that conventional wisdom dictates politicians cannot commit, and the sky did not fall.

Her assault on the "shame" felt by the right wing was, obviously, just one step. For radical conservatism to become the "dominant idea" of our time, it had to triumph in the United States. In the eighteen months that followed Thatcher's rise to power, this would be brought to fruition. Politically, by Ronald Reagan; and, covertly, by the conservative think tanks that skilfully worked the formulas and the ideas that would allow the Republican candidate to win.

Winning this war of ideas was not a foregone conclusion for the American right. There was no guarantee that the American electorate would support reforms that mostly benefited the wealthy. The argument hammered home by Reagan was that the divide was not between those who earned a lot and those who earned much less, but between those who worked for a living and those who sponged off the system. The most powerful image in his speeches was that of the "welfare queen," an utterly fictitious character supposed to represent a woman who lived comfortably, even luxuriously, from welfare benefits without ever having to work. Reagan's description was so realistic that his audience felt that the welfare queen was an actual person; and, according to Paul Krugman, who received the Nobel Prize in Economics, Reagan's words were a dog-whistle message to white voters, particularly in Southern states, who assumed the welfare queen was necessarily a black woman.

Whether the racist intent was real or imagined, there can be no doubt that, for American voters, the image of the welfare queen has resulted in a deep-rooted and enduring mistrust for people they consider emblematic of a welfare system they believe is immoral, one in which money is taken from those who work and given to those who do not. As a result, the rising inequality which has become increasingly stark since the late 1970s—and which, at any other time, might have fuelled a hostility towards the wealthy and a rise in support for left-wing ideas—has simply served to strengthen and entrench conservative opinion in the America of recent decades.

It is not impossible that attitudes will change in the future; but as I write, Ronald Reagan and Margaret Thatcher are still seen by most of their fellow citizens as heroes of a necessary revolution. And the principles they embodied continue to prevail across the world.

*

In the decades that followed, the rise of the Anglo-American conservative ideology at the expense of the left would make the Soviet model seem less attractive and curb its global expansion. But, at the time, it was a series of other setbacks that stalled the momentum of the leaders in Moscow and weakened the Soviet regime.

There were many setbacks, in various parts of the world and in multiple domains—politics, the military, the media, ideology, economics, technology, etc. Below, I mention some that seem more significant than others.

The first occurred in Southeast Asia. The Soviet Union had won a series of dazzling victories, but, in time, those victories triggered a scathing response, and from an unexpected place.

When I mentioned earlier that US-backed regimes in Vietnam, Laos, and Cambodia had fallen like dominoes, I failed to mention that the Communist regimes that subsequently came to power were not all of the same persuasion. While in Vietnam and Laos the victors forged strong ties with the Soviet Union, the Communist regime in Cambodia proclaimed itself Maoist and was led by a curious character who called himself Pol Pot, and who did little to hide his distrust of Hanoi and Moscow. His regime would quickly degenerate into paranoid fanaticism. He began driving citizens out of the capital, Phnom Penh, relentlessly attacked the educated and the cultured and, in four short years, was responsible for one of the most unspeakable genocides in modern history.

As a result, the world felt some relief when the Vietnamese Army launched a brief and effective offensive against the Khmer Rouge, invading the country and occupying Phnom Penh on January 7, 1979. The day before, forces loyal to Pol Pot had deserted the city and retreated to the countryside.

In removing the Khmer Rouge from power, the Vietnamese managed to kill two birds with one stone: they cemented their hegemony in the region, while simultaneously earning plaudits from an international community outraged by the brutality of the regime they had just ousted.

China, however, viewed things differently. There can be no doubt that the new leader, Deng Xiaoping, had little sympathy for the warped Maoism of Pol Pot—or, indeed, for any form of Maoism. But he could not allow the Vietnamese and their Soviet protectors to reign supreme in Southeast Asia and take down Beijing's allies, however ugly and uncontrollable. So, he launched a "punitive mission."

On February 17, 1979, six weeks after the fall of Phnom Penh, 200,000 soldiers of the People's Liberation Army invaded Vietnamese territory and marched southwards, occupying towns and demolishing various economic and military installations along the way. On March 6, China announced that the gate to Hanoi was open, that its troops would go no farther, and that it hoped this would be a "lesson" to Vietnam. For its part, Vietnam claimed to have "repelled the invasion."

If external observers are to be believed, the Vietnamese, seasoned by years of war, fought more fiercely than their enemy, whose army had not fought since the Korean War in the early 1950s. But Deng's objective had not been a military one. Having recently come to power, he was intent on proving that the Soviet Union would not intervene if Vietnam was attacked, and that the Vietnamese were mistaken to think they could act with impunity. He was also sending the message to the United States that it now had a trustworthy ally, perhaps even a potential partner in Asia; the Americans, who had not yet recovered from the defeat inflicted on them by Hanoi, welcomed China's initiative.

An event of great significance had just been played out on the international stage, one that could not but delight Washington, and one that seriously worried Moscow.

4

Another event I would describe as a "setback" for the Soviets—though, at the time, they would probably not have seen it as such—was the murder of Aldo Moro, the leader of Italy's Christian Democracy party, who proposed a "historic compromise" between his party and the Italian Communist Party. On March 16, 1978, he was kidnapped in broad daylight on a street in Rome by the Red Brigades; on May 9, his body was found in the boot of a car.

Even today, after so many years have passed, it is difficult to say for certain who ordered the hit, and to what end. I will not attempt to unravel the number of theories that have been put forward. Were the killers acting on the orders of some secret Italian agency, or of some foreign power, or simply according to their own ideological delusions? Was their goal to prevent the Christian Democracy party offering legitimacy to the Communists and thereby paving a path to power? Or was it, conversely, to prevent the Communists from betraying their Marxist–Leninist ideals? The question has never been resolved.

Today, however, one thing seems certain: this was more than simply the murder of one man; a promising utopia had been thrown into the dustbin of history.

It was an idea that had been in the air for decades. For some, it stemmed from the fear of a nuclear catastrophe, for others from a genuine desire to finally see humanity reconciled, and it was expressed as a question that brimmed with hope: what if, rather than waging brutal wars all over the planet, communism and capitalism could come together and forge a synthesis—one that addressed capitalism's concerns about freedom and democracy, while adopting communism's sense of social justice? Might that not spell the end of the gruelling proxy wars between the blocs, which threatened to destroy humanity?

Such an idea was not fundamentally unreasonable. Indeed, many brilliant minds were drawn to it—writers, philosophers, historians, and a number of political leaders. Among them, Aldo Moro. His country could legitimately aspire to be a pioneer in this field. Italy was not only home to Popes and the centre of the Catholic world, it also boasted the most powerful and most respected Communist Party in the West, one that enjoyed great intellectual prestige. It was led by General Secretary Enrico Berlinguer, a man from the Sardinian nobility rather than the working classes, who publicly favoured multiparty systems and freedom of expression in Eastern Bloc countries. Moro could not hope for a more ideal partner than Berlinguer to realize his dream of a "historic compromise" between the rival ideologies warring over the planet.

But Moro's dream did not appeal to Soviet leaders. When I say that the murder of Aldo Moro was a setback for the Soviets, I am speaking as a belated outside observer who has the luxury of knowing what would occur in the decades that followed and hence knows that the heirs to Lenin were on the brink of a political and moral catastrophe; for the communists of the world, the middle ground advocated by Moro and Berlinguer was not a trap to be avoided, but a last chance to escape the lethal trap about to snap shut on them.

Having said this, I am not entirely convinced that such an opportunity still existed in 1978. Perhaps the Soviet system was already beyond repair—perhaps since the suppression of the Prague Spring in 1968, or since the crushing of the Hungarian uprising in 1956, perhaps even before. What is certain is that, after the failure of the Italian "historic compromise," there would never again be an opportunity for the Cold War to end in a "draw." The defeat of the "socialist camp" was becoming inevitable.

Today everyone knows this; in 1978, the Soviets did not know it.

And yet it was in 1978 that they suffered another major setback. And once again, in the most unlikely of places: Rome.

Earlier I briefly mentioned that October 1978 witnessed the election of a non-Italian pope for the first time in more than four hundred and fifty years. The new pontiff was Polish, and had spent much of his life as a priest under a Soviet-style regime. It is significant that the rise of Pope John Paul II took place when another Pole, one just as hostile to communism, was United States National Security Advisor, tasked with aiding the President to develop and implement his foreign policy.

Zbigniew Brzezinski, known as "Zbig," made no bones about the fact that his origins played a key role in his political vision. When President Jimmy Carter assumed office in 1977, Brzezinski persuaded him that for his first state visit he should visit Warsaw. When they arrived, and despite the protestations of the US Ambassador, Brzezinski insisted on meeting with the Polish prelate of the Roman Catholic Church, Cardinal Wyszyński, the fiercest opponent of the Communist government, whom he assured of his support.

Zbig dreamed of undermining, destabilizing, and ultimately dismantling the empire that the Soviets had built behind the Iron Curtain. Though the goal might have seemed ambitious, it was one to which Brzezinski devoted his considerable passion and skill during the single term of "his" president, and it would be fair to say that the "Polish connection" that existed between Washington and the Vatican during that time helped to loosen the grip of the Russian "Big Brother" on the countries of the Eastern Bloc; especially after the emergence of the Solidarity movement led by Lech Wałęsa in 1980.

*

The presidency of Jimmy Carter is remembered as a period of weakness and indecision. This was how Ronald Reagan portrayed it at the time, a view reinforced by a number of events, notably the capture of the US embassy in Tehran and the humiliating images of blindfolded American hostages.

With hindsight, this impression of weakness has not been borne out, quite the contrary. During the Cold War, the Carter administration had shown no weakness in its dealings with Moscow, but had deployed a strategy that was subtle, discreet, circumspect—and lethally effective. Not least in Afghanistan, where the administration set a deadly trap from which the Soviet Union never managed to extricate itself.

In July 1979, when Afghan communists seized power in Kabul, armed resistance groups were formed to oppose the government in the name of Islam and tradition. Washington reacted by setting up a secret operation, code-named "Cyclone," with the aim of actively supporting the mujahideen rebels. Before this decision was made, a number of US officials expressed concerns that such an operation might lead to Moscow sending troops into Afghanistan. But this prospect did not worry Brzezinski. On the contrary, this was what he expected would happen. He hoped that, being unable to control the situation through local allies, the Soviets would be forced to invade, thereby falling into the trap that he had set—a reverse of the situation in Vietnam—where the Russians would have to play the thankless role of "police" while the United States could fight a proxy war through the rebels.

Brzezinski was extremely proud of this stratagem—but he did not speak about it publicly until the end of the Cold War. "According to the official version of history," he said in a 1998 interview, "CIA aid to the mujahideen began during 1980, that is to say, after the Soviet Army invaded Afghanistan on December 24, 1979. But the reality, closely guarded until now, is completely otherwise: indeed, it was on July 3, 1979 that President Carter signed the first directive for secret aid to the opponents of the pro-Soviet regime in Kabul. And that very day, I wrote a note to the president in which I explained to him that in my opinion this aid was going to induce a Soviet military intervention."

When Vincent Jauvert, interviewing him for *Le Nouvel Observateur*, asked if he regretted anything, he replied: "Regret what? That secret operation was an excellent idea. It had the effect of drawing the Russians into the Afghan trap, and you want me to regret it? The day that the Soviets officially crossed the border, I wrote to President Carter, essentially saying, 'We now have the opportunity of giving the USSR its Vietnam War.' Indeed, for almost ten years, Moscow had to carry on a war that was unsustainable for the regime, a conflict that brought about the demoralization and finally the breakup of the Soviet Empire."

When the White House was informed of the Soviet invasion of Afghanistan, it launched a broad response. Carter announced trade and diplomatic sanctions on the Soviet Union, and called on other countries to boycott the Moscow Olympic Games, scheduled for the summer of 1980.

As the lynchpin in this campaign, Brzezinski set off on a world tour, visiting China and Egypt, Britain and Pakistan, soliciting support from all those troubled by the Soviet invasion. After the initial launch of Operation Cyclone, he secured pledges from several countries, including Saudi Arabia, to provide money, weapons, and men to the mujahideen.

The trickle of foreign combatants, which had begun arriving in Afghanistan a few months earlier, now became a flood, especially from the Arab world. In late 1979, one of those who went to Afghanistan was a twenty-two-year-old Saudi student called Osama bin Laden. Some had gone before him; countless others would follow. In several countries, there were worries about this group of "Afghan Arabs," the armed militia of a new *internationale* that appeared one week on the outskirts of Algiers, and the following week in Sarajevo. But at the time, people believed it was a passing phase, a "collateral effect" of the ongoing war, one that would disappear when the war ended.

Later, when militant Islam began to spread across the globe, directing its vicious attacks at Western targets, many people wondered whether the United States, blinded by its fight against Communism, had not been playing God when it supported emerging forces that would later turn against it. But it is unfair to judge the actions of yesterday based on what we know now. Today, the Soviet Union no longer exists; at the time that it invaded Afghanistan, it possessed a fearsome arsenal in the form of thousands of nuclear warheads capable of destroying the entire planet. The United States had never faced such an enemy, and the goal of every American leader was to counter it, to destabilize it, by any means necessary. They could not allow any other threat to distract them from this primary objective, certainly not the threat—so vague, so remote, so improbable at that time—that, twenty years later, we have come to call violent extremism, or terrorism.

Yet, while it is difficult to blame American leaders for prioritizing all-out war against a rival superpower, it is nonetheless true that it *did* play God by nurturing the emergence of a complex, enigmatic, disconcerting phenomenon that it would later be unable to control.

5

In surveying the broad sweep of the twentieth century, it seems to me that it was the scene of two "families" of catastrophes, one caused by communism, the other by anti-communism.

The former comprises all the atrocities committed in the name of the proletariat, of socialism, of revolution, of progress; these were numerous and they occurred around the world—from the Moscow show trials, to famines in Ukraine, to the abuses in North Korea and the genocide in Cambodia. In the struggle against Bolshevism, too, there are countless tragedies, the most devastating of which was the global cataclysm triggered by the "brown plague" of fascism and Nazism.

How we perceive these different crimes has changed greatly over time. In the immediate aftermath of the Second World War, most historians considered it unwarranted, inappropriate, and even suspect, to equate the crimes of Hitler and those of the Soviet regime. And although the image of Stalin was eventually tarnished, that of his predecessor, Lenin, long remained unscathed.

The reputation of Mao Zedong has also had its ups and downs. Spectacular aberrations, such as the "Great Proletarian Cultural Revolution," were praised at the time by eminent intellectuals, whereas these days, they are roundly condemned. Yet the "Great Helmsman" has not suffered the same fate as the "Father of Nations." There has been no policy of "de-Maoization," and if Mao's successors have carefully steered away from his ideology, they have kept his mausoleum on Tiananmen Square, principally because they see him as a symbol of political continuity and stability.

Only when the Cold War ended, with the collapse of the collectivist model and the breakup of the Soviet Union, did it become acceptable to mock the "little red book," to equate Stalin with Hitler, and to attack the reputation of Lenin. People ceased to see him as the respectable founder of a form of socialism perverted by his successors; he is now seen as bearing much of the responsibility for everything that happened after the October Revolution, which some historians paint as little more than a crude coup d'état—daring, granted, but certainly not a popular uprising.

This is not particularly surprising; it is a fitting reversal. More than any other ideology, communism had its chance and squandered it. It could have championed its ideals; instead it discredited them. For far too long, communism was treated too leniently; now, we judge it harshly.

After this shift in perspective, can we conclude that our vision of the crimes of the twentieth century is now fair and balanced? Not quite, unfortunately. When it comes to the atrocities committed by Communist regimes, old obfuscations and illusions have been swept away. The same is true of the atrocities committed by the Nazis, the Fascists, and their fellow travellers in the 1930s and 1940s. So, although historians will continue to research, to deliberate, to relate, and to interpret, it is reasonable to consider that our overall picture of the first half of the twentieth century essentially tallies with what actually occurred.

However, when it comes to the crimes committed during the Cold War, from the 1940s to the early 1990s, the picture is at best incomplete, and often downright warped. In the aftermath of World War II, was there not a tacit acceptance of the atrocities committed by the victors—those of Stalin, obviously, but also the mass killings perpetrated by the West in Dresden or Hiroshima? The end of the Cold War has resulted in a similar situation. While no one any longer casts doubt on the horrors committed by Marxist–Leninist regimes—in Hungary, in Ethiopia, in Cambodia, in Cuba—those committed in the name of the fight against communism are considered, if not as a necessary "surgical procedure," then as "collateral damage," regrettable but unavoidable, and carried out in pursuit of a just cause.

What I have just said requires a little qualification. Such a lenient approach is not systematic. For example, the brutal repression of Marxists by right-wing dictatorships, like that of Pinochet in Chile, or that carried out by the military regimes in Argentina and Brazil, is widely denounced. And the "witch hunt" conducted by Senator Joseph McCarthy in the 1950s is a recurring theme in American films and novels. But, when it comes to the crimes committed in the name of anti-communism or against leaders in the Muslim world, our consciences are dulled.

*

Earlier, I mentioned the Communist Party of Indonesia, and pointed out that when I was a child it was the largest in the world after China and the Soviet Union. Between 1965 and 1966, it was brutally and systematically wiped out in a series of large-scale killings that resulted in the deaths of at least half a million people, and probably many more. Managers, teachers, students, artists, and trade unionists were ruthlessly butchered, often with their families. In 2017, the CIA made public documents that confirmed what researchers already knew, namely that the United States had actively participated in the killings, and even provided the death squads with lists of people to be eliminated.

Just as serious as the massacres themselves was the complete annihilation of an intellectual elite with modernist and secular aspirations, which left this great Muslim country in the hands of a corrupt military and faced with increasingly extremist religious militants. The term "genocide" is reserved for the systematic slaughter of a particular group—a people, an ethnic group, a religious community. No equivalent exists to describe the slaughter of millions of people who share a particular ideology. But the terminology matters little ... What the West destroyed in Indonesia, in the name of the fight against communism, was the opportunity for the largest Muslim country to now have a future based on modernity, progress, diversity, pluralism.

Yet, despite the enormity and the terrible consequences of this crime, it has never generated particular outrage across the world; and its perpetrators—whether Indonesian or American—were never investigated. It was simply written off.

This is not the only example. In the 1950s, Iran suffered a similar catastrophe, when the patriotic regime of Mohammad Mosaddegh, who championed modernist and democratic ideals, and whose claims that Iran should have a greater share in oil revenue were a matter of basic justice, was overthrown in a coup d'état orchestrated by the American and British secret services— again, these are not allegations, but proven facts for which there is documentary evidence, and which those responsible do not even seek to deny.

On the pretext that there were a number of Marxists in

Mosaddegh's entourage, the coup was presented as an episode in the fight against communism; in fact, the sole reason for the coup was to carry on the shameless looting of oil revenues, leaving only crumbs for the local population. The consequence, as we now know, was to pave the way for an Islamic revolution that was radically hostile to the West.

These are just two of the many examples of the counterproductive effects of anti-communist activities in the Arab-Muslim world during the Cold War. Wherever they occurred, they undermined the opportunity for social and political development, and wherever they occurred they fuelled resentment and paved the way for fanaticism and obscurantism.

I am reminded of these facts whenever I hear someone pontificate that Muslim societies, by virtue of their nature and their religion, are inimical to secularism and to modernity. Such post hoc arguments are neither relevant nor true. To my mind, it is how human societies develop that determines how they read sacred texts. And it is the vicissitudes of history that determine how people live and interpret their beliefs.

Earlier, I said that Communist regimes spent a long time discrediting precisely those universal ideas they professed to support. I feel obliged to add that Western powers have also dangerously discredited their own ideals. Not because they fought a fierce struggle with their Marxist opponents or their proxies in the Third World— no one can blame them for that; but because they have cynically exploited the noblest universal principles in the service of their ambitions and their greed; and, more than that, because, particularly in the Arab world, they have constantly made allies of the most reactionary, the most obscurantist forces, the very forces that would one day declare an all-out war on them.

The pitiful spectacle of the world in this century is the result of all these moral failures, these betrayals.

6

All too often in recent years, I have found that the word which spontaneously comes to me is "regression." When we hear about a grotesque beheading, a group of school-girls reduced to slavery, an ancient monument being blown up, or the resurgence of hateful ideologies we thought banished forever, do we not think of moral regression?

But the concept is inadequate. And though I still use it occasionally out of impatience, out of rage and spite, I know the term is crude and rather misleading. We are not really going back to the Stone Age, or the Middle Ages, to the horrors of the Inquisition, to the 1930s, or even to the Cold War; that is not how history works. It is impossible to go back, impossible to return to the physical or mental circumstances of an earlier age. Time's arrow invariably takes us into unexplored, un-charted territories—areas which only superficially re-semble those experienced by previous generations.

Even the most reactionary or antiquated behaviours can only be interpreted in the context of today; their link to the past is an illusion. A "Golden Age" is invariably a post hoc myth created to serve some political or ideologi-cal project. And this is also true of all the most powerful moments in human history, whether they are seen as idyllic or tragic.

It is with this in mind that I look back on the reversal that occurred around 1979, when diverse conservative forces raised the banner of revolution, and advocates of prog-ress were forced onto the defensive.

When I first mentioned this phenomenon I said that,

paradoxical as they were, these "revolutions" could not simply be brushed aside as illegitimate, or fictitious. Nor could they simply be dismissed as a regression. Regardless of the indignation or the concern they might arouse in me and in many of my contemporaries, they nonetheless represent a major phenomenon of our time and therefore deserve to be studied judiciously and intelligently, making a careful distinction between their benefits and their pernicious effects—a distinction that is not always easy to make.

These revolutions were accompanied by significant changes in the attitudes of my contemporaries. Perhaps the most notable of these is the attitude to the role of government in the economy.

There are few people who still tout the virtues of interventionism, or who question the importance of market forces. Most politicians now believe in the importance of freeing businesses and businessmen of the red tape that hinders them.

Britain and the United States, the two Western countries that pioneered the conservative revolution, wanted "freedom" from the welfare state, namely from the tendency of government to steadily raise taxes and increase social benefits in order to reduce the gap between rich and poor. In China, on the other hand, and in other countries that had attempted to apply the precepts of "scientific socialism," what people wanted was freedom from the centralized, dogmatic, and bureaucratic management of the economy, which consistently led to inefficiency, corruption, demoralization, and chronic shortages. Understandably, the goals of Deng Xiaoping were not the same as those of Margaret Thatcher or Ronald Reagan; nonetheless there were certain points on which they agreed, since all three shared the goal of building a dynamic, more streamlined, more productive, and more competitive economy.

While Washington and London were responsible for imposing the primacy of market forces on the rest of the world, it would be foolish to underestimate the iconic role played by the meteoric success of China.

For decades, many countries in what was called the "Third World" were drawn to state socialism, which promised to lift them out of underdevelopment by means other than those of the West. Many leaders in Asia, Africa, and Latin America embraced the idea, hoping to distinguish themselves from the former colonial powers and the United States. Within a few years, all would discover that the system did not work, that it did not keep its promises, that it had led them to the brink of ruin.

At this point, they found themselves in a dilemma; they knew they had taken the wrong path, but did not dare admit it and did not know how to get out. Only after the largest communist country in the world embraced the market economy and, in doing so, pulled off one of the most staggering miracles in human history, was it clear that scientific socialism was definitely obsolete.

For years, the two ideologies had brutally fought it out in the ring, until the Chinese referee, Deng Xiaoping, raised the arm of capitalism and proclaimed it the winner.

*

In reassessing the impact of the transformations brought about by the conservative revolutions, it would be wrong to simply dismiss them as a regression. In many ways, they have been truly revolutionary.

Before this, capitalism had neither the wisdom nor the willingness to share its expertise and its dynamism with major partners from other cultures. Now, suddenly, within a few decades, a revolution flying the banner for a different type of "freedom"— the free flow of trade and capital—began to redress a centuries-old injustice. The skills and expertise of the industrialised West spread across the world, radically transforming the physical and human landscape of the planet. One after another, the great nations of the southern hemisphere determinedly adopted a path that would lead them out of underdevelopment and its attendant plagues: ignorance, incompetence, malnutrition, ill-health, and epidemics.

It is a long road, admittedly, but we now know that those who are left behind will be those without the will or the wisdom to move forward, to adapt, to build.

We need shed no tears for the defunct interventionist system. Everywhere it was implemented, it failed to keep its promises: in the former Third World and in the former Socialist Bloc. Everywhere, it proved ineffective; everywhere, it pandered to authoritarian tendencies and the rise of repressive and parasitic "elites." It has met the fate that it deserved, it has been tossed forever into the proverbial dustbin of history.

The problem is that this particular brand of socialism, however inept or misguided, was not the only ideology to suffer. In accordance with a law frequently observed in human societies, when a project, an ideology, an institution, or a person fails, everything connected to it is also tainted.

The standard-bearers of the conservative revolution did not simply manage to discredit communism, but also social democracy, and with it all the ideologies that had shown themselves accommodating to the ideals of socialism, even if only to fight it from within.

It was not just the excesses of egalitarianism that were denounced; the very principle of equality was devalued and called into question. In the United States, the gap between rich and poor, having steadily decreased since the 1930s, suddenly began to soar in the late 1970s, and, by the early twenty-first century, levels of inequality are comparable to those of the nineteenth century. This has led some people to justifiably argue that—at least in terms of equality—what we are experiencing is indeed a relapse.

Nor did the vanguard of the conservative revolution simply denounce the abuses of bureaucracy; it fostered a culture of distrust and denigration towards public authorities, as though any government intervention in the economy was necessarily an "encroachment," to be resisted by honest citizens. To quote a powerful line from Ronald Reagan's inaugural address: "In this present crisis, government is not the solution to our problem, *government is the problem.*"

This sentence has been much discussed ever since. It has been analysed, interpreted, dissected, and sometimes wisely returned to the precise context in which it was uttered. But it undeniably reflects a mindset that embodies the unrepentant conservative activism of which the former president was the standard-bearer, and which, in our era, has spread across the globe and has now become the norm.

7

For all of the reasons I have cited, I find it difficult to formulate a clear-cut opinion of the changes brought about by the conservative revolution, not only in managing the economy, but in the relationship between a government and its citizens. On the one hand, it has fostered social division and has resulted in terrible injustices; but on the other it has facilitated the meteoric rise of major developing countries and their access to advanced technology, which is unquestionably a step forward.

The consequences seem to me to be sufficiently complex and mixed that I cannot bring myself to simply say that this reversal in economic policies has resulted in an out-and-out regression; something that I do not hesitate to do when it comes to the other transformation brought about by the conservative revolutions. I am referring to the steady, generalized increase in identity-based tensions that has spread like a drug through the veins of our contemporaries, and now affects all human societies.

It cannot be said for certain that the explosion in identity politics is a *direct result* of the conservative revolutions, but it would be fair to say that there has been a *synchronicity* between the two phenomena.

But this was no accident. Because identity has always been a powerful part of the discourse of those who traditionally advocate conservatism—often rooted in religion, citizenship, land, culture, race, or a mixture of the above. It can be found among Republicans in the United States, the Israeli nationalists in Likud, Indian nationalists in the BJP, the Taliban in Afghanistan, the mullahs of Iran, and more broadly in every political faction that has been waging its own conservative revolution since the 1970s.

Which once again brings me back to 1979, a year I have called "the year of the great reversal." The resolutely rational observer in me refuses to credit this number with any secret power; it recurs simply because significant events took place in or around that year, events that marked a turning point, or sometimes a watershed moment in history. Surely there are simply years like this, dates that become *a bookmark in the great ledger of time*, dates that signal the end of one chapter and the beginning of another? To my mind, 1979 is one such year. At the time I was thirty years old and, although I felt the earth move under my feet, I did not realize the magnitude of the quake.

That year marked a significant change in the long turbulent history of identity politics with the sudden emergence of a paradoxical form of Islamism, one that was socially traditionalist but politically radical and, though we did not know it then, one whose insurrectionary power would have devastating consequences. The Islamic Republic of Iran was founded in February 1979 amid the ruins of a monarchy it considered too modernist and too westernized; in April 1979, the former president of Pakistan, Zulfikar Ali Bhutto, was hanged, having been sentenced to death by military putschists who accused him of advocating socialism and secularism, and demanded the strict application of Islamic law; in July 1979 came the US decision to secretly arm the Islamist mujahideen in Afghanistan; in November 1979, an impressive commando of Saudi Islamist militants seized the Grand Mosque in Mecca in an operation that would end in a bloodbath; in December 1979, Soviet troops marched into Afghanistan, and it was against them that modern jihadism would wage its first war ...

It goes without saying that each of these events had its

own causes. Nonetheless, the rate at which such events occurred seemed to presage a new reality—something that is confirmed in hindsight. Many of the iconic moments that have shaped our era, from the fall of the Berlin Wall to the collapse of the World Trade Center in Manhattan, have their roots in the events of that year ...

Once again, I should stress that there is no *single* common explanation for all these incidents. At random, one could cite the overconfidence of the Soviet leadership after its successes in Southeast Asia and sub-Saharan Africa; the profound distress felt in the Arab world after the defeat of 1967 and Nasser's death; the shift in how America saw its role in the Cold War; the subterranean fault lines within Muslim societies; and many other reasons besides.

However, one factor deserves closer scrutiny than the others: the oil crisis. The crisis took the form of a series of shocks that rippled through the 1970s, and which would radically change a number of economic, social, and political considerations across the world; they would lead to a drastic shift both in attitudes and in the balance of power; they would spread throughout Arab world, and, from there, across the planet in a dense cloud of obscurantism and reactionary attitudes.

*

The main "shock" came when the oil-producing countries proclaimed an oil embargo in protest at the US military aid provided to Israel in its war against Egypt and Syria in October 1973. The embargo did not last long, but the significant increase in the price of crude oil, which until then had been extremely low, would have a painful impact on importing countries for years to come.

There can be no doubt that this incident played a decisive role in the events that led to the various conservative revolutions. For example, it we look at the situation in Britain on the eve of Margaret Thatcher's victory, it is clear that the crisis afflicting the country was largely related to energy, one of the most symbolic events having been the blackout at Piccadilly Circus. The conservative leader promised to put an end to such disruptions.

This is exactly what Ronald Reagan would do some months later, on the other side of the Atlantic. While President Carter was calling on his fellow citizens to reduce energy consumption so that the country would not be dependent on oil imports and consequently forced to engage in foreign wars to protect supplies, the Republican candidate adopted the opposite approach, telling American consumers not to change their habits, and pledging to do whatever was needed—even if it involved the use of force—to avoid consumers having to tighten their belts.

It was the latter message that voters wanted to hear, as was confirmed by the election results. Appealing to the national pride of the American people and their desire not to change their consumption proved more appealing than calling for a sense of moderation that smacked of surrender.

The oil-importing countries, whether rich or poor, all went through a turbulent period before they could adapt to the new economic reality caused by the rise in oil prices. These years of doubt and uncertainty were stressful, and even traumatic. But it was in the oil-exporting countries that the most spectacular aftershocks were seen. Triggered by the overweening ambition of some Arab leaders and insatiable expectations generated in the populace by the sudden influx of petrodollars, the aftershocks quickly began, and they have never stopped.

The Shah of Iran, one of the chief architects of the "oil crisis," was ousted in February 1979 after a popular uprising. Shortly afterwards, there was a major political upheaval in Saudi Arabia, one that many contemporary observers dismissed as a bizarre, isolated incident, but which would go on to have global consequences—I will come back to this. As for Iraq, its subsequent history was little more than a succession of invasions and counter-invasions, of wars and massacres that left the country ruined and on its knees. One has only to look at "fortunate" beneficiaries of this manna to be reminded of the tragedies brought about by the trade in black gold. In addition to those already mentioned, the list might include Libya, Algeria, Indonesia, Kuwait, Nigeria, or Venezuela ...

A sombre wreath of the tragedies of our age ...

*

Within the Arab world, the most immediate consequence of the oil crisis was that those countries exporting the precious commodity found themselves in possession of vast liquid assets, which gave them an advantage over those without similar natural resources. Egypt lost the dominant position it had occupied under Nasser; overnight, Saudi Arabia emerged as a major player; the leaders of Iraq and Libya, Saddam Hussein and Muammar Gaddafi, began to imagine themselves as the leaders of the Arab nation, and squandered much of their newfound wealth in the service of this ambition, to no avail.

A more enduring effect of this shift in power was the

shift in attitudes and in intellectual discourse. The ideologies that had previously prevailed, inspired by nationalism, by socialism, or modelled on Western societies, were gradually eclipsed by others which came from desert countries that had long been isolated from the main currents of political thought. On the political stage, a curious group of new actors appeared: young men raised in conservative environments, many of them with considerable wealth, who were willing to spend money in order to spread the faith.

Today, everyone knows the name Osama bin Laden, together with a handful of others who ordered or committed spectacular terrorist attacks. But hundreds of thousands, perhaps millions of anonymous young men contributed to the wars in Afghanistan, in Bosnia, and elsewhere, without having set foot in the country, simply by sending their money to some collector, convinced it was a pious act. At the time, many Arabs felt humiliated and disoriented, orphaned from their heroes, and betrayed, not only by their leaders, but by the "modern" ideologies in which they had believed. They were ripe to rally under the banner of religion.

When Brzezinski came to ask America's allies—including Saudi Arabia, Egypt, and Pakistan—to send money and weapons to the mujahideen in Afghanistan, and for volunteers who were prepared to fight the infidel communists, his speech did not fall on deaf ears.

His strategy happened to be in lockstep with the jihadist aspirations that had rocked a certain sector of the populace. It also chimed with the concerns of leaders in the region, who, like the Americans, were concerned by the Soviet threat, but at the same time were even more alarmed by the nationalist and Islamist popular uprisings which had already overthrown the Shah of Iran and which, they feared, might topple all the monarchies in the region.

8

The vagaries of my life as a journalist meant that during the Iranian revolution I was once again witness to one of the great upheavals of my age.

I use the term "witness" in its most literal sense: when the foundation of the Islamic Republic was announced, I was in a small theatre in Tehran; on the stage in front of me, sitting in a large armchair before the curtain, was Ayatollah Khomeini. It was February 5, 1979, and this strange picture is forever imprinted on my memory.

I was now living in Paris and was once again working as a journalist, though I now wrote in French rather than Arabic, and I spent my time covering the Arab-Muslim world rather than the rest of the planet.

I had watched in fascination when, in the summer of 1978, mass demonstrations had erupted in Iran, threatening the Shah's throne. A revolution led by a sixty-six-year-old religious leader with a black turban and white beard was hardly a common sight in the last quarter of the twentieth century. Like many of my contemporaries, I followed the unfolding events with more disbelief than concern. The Iranian people viewed the monarchy as repressive, corrupt, and profligate; they were not interested in its programme of modernization.

At the beginning of the unrest, Khomeini was living in exile in southern Iraq, in a place revered by Shia Muslims throughout the world. But the Shah of Iran demanded that he be expelled, and Saddam Hussein asked the Ayatollah to seek asylum elsewhere—something the Ayatollah would never forgive. France offered to take in its erstwhile opponent, and for a few months, Neauphle-le-Château, a small town near Paris, became the unlikely headquarters of the Iranian revolution.

I visited two or three times, and had the opportunity to interview Khomeini, with a young Lebanese Shiite cleric, who was part of his entourage, kindly accepting to act as interpreter. I phrased my questions in classical Arabic; Khomeini evidently understood me and sometimes responded with a nod, but he answered in Farsi, and the interpreter whispered the translation to me. All three of us were sitting on thick cushions on a floor covered with Persian rugs.

I also talked with some of the men in the leader's inner circle, who, naturally, held him in great esteem, without necessarily sharing all of his ideas. The most important of them was Ebrahim Yazdi, a biochemist who would later be appointed minister for foreign affairs in the first Islamic Republic government before falling out of favour and becoming a leading figure in the opposition to the Ayatollahs.

It was he who telephoned me on January 31 to say that Air France had chartered an aircraft so that Khomeini could return to Iran. There was room for the Ayatollah and his entourage, and for foreign journalists who wished to cover the event. Yazdi asked whether I would be willing to make the trip. I promised to meet him two hours before takeoff, which was scheduled for midnight.

At Tehran airport, officials greeted the Ayatollah with frosty solemnity, but out in the streets he was greeted by a crowd of people larger than I had never seen. It was as if the entire population had turned out to welcome him.

It was a triumph, even if his standing in the country at large was still unclear. He was not in power, and his family still feared elements within the army might attack him. But no one else was running the country. The rival camp was in utter disarray.

During this interim period, Khomeini set up temporary headquarters in a public school in an area where his supporters could protect him. Demonstrators protesting against the existing regime thronged the neighbouring streets, and Khomeini would often go out onto the balcony to greet them.

After three days, he decided that the time was ripe for advancing his first pawn on the board. He organized a small event in a cinema, for close family, a few politicians, and religious leaders, together with the foreign journalists who had come with him from France.

And so, Khomeini was onstage, seated in an armchair. On his left stood Mehdi Bazargan, a man in a sober suit and tie who was barely younger than he was. There and then, the Ayatollah appointed Bazargan to lead the government of the new republic. The Islamic Republic of Iran was born right before our eyes. Elsewhere in Tehran, there was still an existing government, one appointed by the Shah and led by Shapour Bakhtiar. But it was clear that the old regime would be gone within a matter of days, perhaps even hours.

The place he had chosen for the announcement was in stark contrast to the magnitude of the event. An empire that had endured for more than a thousand years had been abolished before our eyes; the Muslim world was in the throes of an upheaval that would have consequences for the planet as a whole. But the atmosphere was like a village hall, and the ceremony itself like a school presentation; it felt like an end-of-year prize-giving, with an award for the most promising pupil. Bazargan merely reinforced this impression. Excited and excitable, clearly nervous in his pale, hastily buttoned suit, he clutched the crumpled pages of his acceptance speech; he looked as though he did not want to be on the stage, and could not wait to get off it.

By reputation, Bazargan was honest and competent, and his appointment as prime minister did much to reassure those who hoped the Khomeini revolution would lead Iran towards becoming a modern democratic state. He had been primarily educated in France, at a lycée in Nantes and later at the École Centrale in Paris, where he obtained a degree in engineering.

In 1951, when Mosaddegh had sought to retake control of Iranian oil production, he had picked Bazargan to head up the National Iranian Oil Company. Although the venture ended tragically two years later with the CIA-orchestrated coup d'état, the memory of it was still very much alive, and the fact that the new revolution should call on one of the leaders of the previous revolution was encouraging.

Equally reassuring was the appointment of Yazdi as deputy prime minister. Two men of science, renowned for their integrity, their modern outlook, and their democratic convictions were to lead the government. Those who believed that Khomeini would be a benign, good-natured grandfather to the nation could not but rejoice. The revolution, it seemed, had got off to the most auspicious start.

*

It is reasonable to assume that, from the outset, the Ayatollah had very different plans. Plans that were much more ambitious, certainly, but much less reassuring to those hoping for a smooth transition from monarchy to republic. To his heirs, he would bequeath a regime of a very different kind, one that was socially conservative and politically radical. Under his direction, Iran would be transformed into a dynamic regional power whose style was eccentric, whose pronouncements carried weight, whose initiatives were respected, but one constantly involved in titanic struggles that were never truly lost or won and never came to an end.

One of the most noteworthy early changes was the abrupt reversal of Iranian policy regarding the Middle East conflict. The Shah had forged friendly relations with Israel, and supplied the country with oil, something other Arab nations had refused to do. Khomeini immediately put an end to this practice and broke off diplomatic relations, he welcomed Arafat to Tehran before any other foreign leader, and he even allowed the PLO to use the buildings that had previously housed the Israeli diplomatic service. In the early months of the revolution, there was an influx of Palestinian political and military advisers.

But, though it may have seemed promising, the relationship between the two countries did not get off on the right foot. The proud, fiercely nationalist Iranians saw little point in bringing in a cohort of Arab advisors, while, for his part, Arafat worried that closer ties with Iran might sour his relationship with Saddam Hussein and Iraq at a time when he was already embroiled in a trial of strength with Assad in Syria.

This honeymoon with the PLO proved fleeting, but Tehran's engagement in the Arab–Israeli conflict carried on. In fact, it came to represent a major strategic asset to Iran's mullahs.

The most surprising factor—one that could not have been predicted, but one that would have major consequences—was that, despite not being Arabic, revolutionary Iran adopted a discourse similar to that of Arab nationalism, particularly on the subject of Palestine and the conflict with Israel.

This positioning would bear fruit. The Islamic Republic would have a decisive influence over many Middle Eastern countries, including Iraq and Syria; it would sponsor armed movements such as Hezbollah in Lebanon, Hamas and Islamic Jihad in Gaza, and the Houthi in Yemen; and it would have a significant presence in Afghanistan, as in a number of former Soviet republics.

But this increase in power was marked by a visceral outburst of mutual hatred between Sunni Muslims, who represented the majority in most Arab countries, and Shia Muslims, who were the majority in Iran. It was a conflict that had been dormant for centuries, and might otherwise have remained so. As I have already said, in the Beirut of my youth, the distinction seemed of little import. It is true that the Shiites in Lebanon were more likely to live in disadvantaged areas; but this resulted in their joining left-wing parties and working-class movements, rather than simply demanding their rights in the name of their religion. I realize I am talking about a bygone era, one where people had a very different perception of identity, where people thought differently, and where people acted according to different criteria.

Since then, the zeitgeist has changed how people behave—this drift cannot simply be blamed on one protagonist while exculpating the other. That said, there is little doubt that in seeking a leading role in an Arab world which was predominantly Sunni, and relying on the support of local Shia communities to attain it, Iran risked provoking hostile reactions. From those regimes it threatened, like Saudi Arabia, and, more generally, from the Sunni population, who felt cheated, threatened, and marginalized by the Shiites' growing influence.

Even among radical Sunni elements, which were fiercely opposed to the oil monarchies and would have happily seen them swept aside by an Islamist revolution, as the Shah of Iran had been, the barriers of community proved extremely difficult to cross. Although Sunni radicals may have admired those who had managed to overthrow the Pahlavi dynasty, while they had been powerless to topple their own ruling dynasties, they never forgot that this feat had been achieved by "schismatics," and they were determined to prove that adherents to the "true tradition of the Prophet" could do better.

9

This aspect certainly played a role in the drift that the Arab world has experienced in recent decades, one that has now affected the entire planet. In fact, it has resulted in a kind of competition between various factions, all of which present themselves as the standard-bearers of "the holy war against the enemies of Islam." This is not only the case between Sunnis and Shiites, but also among various Sunni militant factions.

One of the most terrifying examples has been the bloody campaign waged by the so-called "Islamic State" in seeking to replace Al-Qaeda as the dominant force in the jihadist movement; the "challenger" has resorted to acts of unspeakable violence, notably public beheadings, to prove that it is prepared to plumb new depths of horror, to go beyond what others will do, in order to attract the most fanatical militants to its cause.

As insane as it may sound, there is Machiavellian logic to such behaviour. Surely this is precisely how brinkmanship works? When one "contender" goes too far in its brutality or its cruelty, its rivals cannot follow and are forced to leave the field open.

The case I mention is one of the most sickening, but it is only one among many in a very long and deeply twisted "competition."

An earlier example of this competitive spirit took place in the last weeks of 1979—that year again! On Sunday, November 4, hundreds of Iranian students seized the US embassy in Tehran and took fifty-two hostages in what they called a "revolutionary occupation." Sixteen days later, on November 20, hundreds of Sunni jihadists from Saudi Arabia seized the Grand Mosque in Mecca.

If the first of these attacks was extraordinary, the second was even more unprecedented. Armed commando units occupying the holiest place of Islam! And demanding the enforcement of Sharia law at a time when, in the eyes of the world, Saudi Arabia was seen as the epitome of a country governed by harsh religious laws! To make matters worse, this was not a single commando unit that had slipped past the guards: it was a small army, with vehicles and heavy artillery!

More surprising still was the reaction of the Saudi authorities. It was expected that they would swiftly move to restore order. But they seemed helpless, paralysed, powerless. They were forced to call on allies, including Pakistan and France, to send elite units to advise and support local troops. Only after a pitched battle lasting two weeks was the mosque eventually retaken. An estimated three hundred people died. Sixty-eight rebels were captured and later beheaded.

This unprecedented attack in Islam's holiest city was the beginning of a radical Sunni militancy that would continue for decades. At the time, many of those who admired the daring commando raid, and felt crushed that it had been defeated, left the Arabian Peninsula to carry on the fight elsewhere. In Afghanistan, for example. And the Saudi government, anxious to be rid of them, encouraged them to go. Such was the case with Osama bin Laden; it was after this that he began building the powerful global jihadist network that would take the name of Al-Qaeda—"The Foundation"—which became infamous for a series of devastating terrorist attacks, culminating in the attack on New York's Twin Towers on September 11, 2001.

Another major consequence of the incident in Mecca

was to undermine Saudi Arabia and thereby prompt its leaders to radically change their approach to religious issues. Some observers interested in the history of the kingdom talk about the "trauma of 1979," after which the Saudi regime, fearful it might seem weak in its defence of the faith, redoubled its efforts to spread Wahhabism and Salafism around the world, by building mosques and financing religious associations in Dakar, in Jakarta, and in the West ... Even the form of address for the king was changed; no longer was he referred to as His Majesty, for majesty was the preserve of the Creator—thereafter, in all acts of government and in both official and unofficial media, the monarch was known as the "Custodian of the Two Holy Mosques," namely Mecca and Medina.

Doubtless, in adopting the title, the kingdom felt it was issuing a "certificate" of piety, which might protect it from the brinkmanship at play. But that is not what happened. It is a fallacy to think that by being radical, one will silence the radicals. What happens is often the reverse. A regime such as that in Saudi Arabia, which to the world may seem strictly traditionalist, is rife with internal factions that use protestations of orthodoxy to accuse it of being insufficiently Islamic. Its teachings legitimize a particular view of the world which others are quick to turn against it.

For decades, the Saudi monarchy found itself prisoner of a rhetoric it had helped to propagate, and from which it could not extricate itself without jeopardizing the very foundations on which the kingdom was built. The trauma caused by the bloody events of 1979 would prove long-lasting.

*

The "revolutionary students" who stormed the American Embassy in Tehran experienced a different fate to those who occupied the Grand Mosque in Mecca. Although Ayatollah Khomeini did not publicly express approval for their actions, he carefully refrained from condemning them, and even expressed his sympathy by describing the building they had stormed as a "nest of spies." Far from being chastened, they were hailed as heroes, and many went on to play important roles in later years. The attitude of the Supreme Leader of the Islamic Revolution deeply disappointed both Bazargan and Yazdi, who immediately resigned from office. Their departure marked the end of any illusions for those who believed that the Islamic Republic might evolve into a liberal democracy.

The occupation of the embassy lasted for almost fifteen months, and significantly influenced the ongoing American presidential election. Humiliated at the images of handcuffed and blindfolded US diplomats, American voters resented President Carter for failing to act, all the more so when a commando operation intended to free the hostages went spectacularly wrong. Ronald Reagan, the Republican candidate, made the most of this, lambasting the Democratic administration for its weakness and incompetence.

The embassy siege decisively contributed to Carter's crushing defeat. So much so that there have been persistent allegations that Reagan's envoys held talks with Iranian representatives in Paris and asked to postpone any settlement until after the election. No doubt, historians will continue to debate what actually happened for many years to come. However, as though to lend credence to the allegations, the Iranian government chose to announce the release of the hostages on January 20, 1981, the day Reagan took office, during his inauguration ceremony in Washington.

The new US administration did not appear particularly hostile towards the Islamic Republic. In fact, during Reagan's second term, a huge scandal erupted when Congress discovered that the White House was illegally funding anti-Sandinista guerrillas in Nicaragua, using money amassed through illegal arms trading to the *Pasdaran*—the Islamic Revolutionary Guard.

While the operation, dubbed the "Iran–Contra Affair" or "Irangate," was certainly cynical, devious, and hugely complicated, it would be rash to conclude that there was any active collusion between the two conservative revolutions in Washington and Tehran. I see it rather as a point of convergence, born of the constraints of the time. It was a different era, with a different international atmosphere, different power relations, different priorities. In Reagan's eyes, Communism was still Enemy Number One; all other conflicts seemed secondary and ephemeral.

But the placid explanation I have just given is not unanimously accepted. Many in the Arab world, especially among Sunni Muslims, are absolutely convinced that there is collusion between the Islamic Republic and the United States. Although there are constant chants of "Death to America!" in Tehran, and although Washington accuses Iran of being a "state sponsor" of all forms of terrorism, there are some who still believe there are tacit, clandestine links between the Shiites and the United States.

This suspicion dates from the Iraq War in 2003. Sunnis in Iraq accused Shiites of having driven them from power with the complicity of the American invaders. They immediately launched a series of heavy attacks against Shiite targets, including mosques, processions of pilgrims, and gatherings of the faithful, which were masterminded by a Jordanian jihadist nicknamed "Al-Zarqawi," who had cut his teeth in Afghanistan.

A cycle of violence would sweep through many Muslim countries, one that had all the hallmarks of a sectarian war; one that would culminate in the rise of that grim entity known as the "Islamic State"; one that would reinforce this idea that the Arab world had regressed to the darkest periods of its past.

IV

A Decaying World

We were made to understand it would be
Terrible. Every small want, every niggling urge,
Every hate swollen to a kind of epic wind.

Livid the land, and ravaged, like a rageful
Dream. The worst in us having taken over
And the rest broken utterly down.

Tracy K. Smith (born 1972)
"An Old Story"

1

At the close of the twentieth century, it was predicted that the world would henceforth be marked by a "clash of civilizations," particularly between religions. As disturbing as it was, the prediction has not been disproved by the facts. Where the prediction was wrong was in assuming that this "clash" between different cultures would reinforce cohesion within each. In fact, the opposite has happened. Humanity today is characterized, not by a tendency for people to coalesce in vast groups, but by a tendency to fragment and to splinter, often violently and acrimoniously.

This is clearly evidenced in the Arab-Muslim world, which seems to have taken it upon itself to harbour all the ills of our times and to amplify them to an absurd degree. While the hostility between the Arab world and the rest of the planet has continued to rise, it is inside the Arab world that the most brutal rifts have occurred, as evidenced by the countless bloody conflicts that have taken place in recent decades, in Afghanistan and in Mali, in Lebanon, in Syria, Iraq, Libya, Yemen, Sudan, Nigeria, and Somalia.

Granted, this is an extreme case. We have not seen the same breakdown in other "areas of civilization," but this tendency towards fragmentation and tribalism is visible everywhere. It can be seen in American society—which has led some malicious minds to talk about the "Disunited States." It can be seen in the European Union, which has been shaken by Brexit and by the crises and the tensions provoked by migration. It is acute in older countries; unions that have existed for centuries and once boasted sweeping empires—in Catalonia, in Scotland,

and elsewhere—are now facing forceful and determined independence movements.

There is obviously no single, unified explanation for these fragmentations. Nonetheless, if we look beyond specific local circumstances, we can detect a similar impulse, one clearly connected to the zeitgeist. In particular, I feel that within our societies, and within humanity as a whole, there are, increasingly, more factors that divide and fewer that bind. One of the things that has aggravated this tendency is the fact that the world is filled with "false bonds," for example the religious bonds that claim to unite mankind when in fact they do the reverse.

Before discussing what has become of human solidarity, I feel I should mention an idea that has had a decisive influence on contemporary attitudes, though it dates back to eighteenth-century Scotland: that each person should act according to his own self-interest, and that the sum of these self-interested actions is necessarily advantageous to society as a whole; as though an "invisible hand" providentially intervenes to balance our actions—a subtle, complex, and mysterious process beyond the capabilities of government, which should therefore not intervene, since governmental intervention would complicate rather than facilitate the process.

First formulated by the economist Adam Smith in *The Wealth of Nations*, published in 1776, this idea once again became topical in the late 1970s and has significantly influenced contemporary attitudes. It is not difficult to imagine its political implications, and its appeal to those who distrust the role of the State in regulating the economy and redistributing wealth; it is hardly surprising, then, that the supporters of the conservative revolutions of Thatcher and Reagan appropriated the idea, and indeed saw it as the very basis for their worldview.

Such a theory may seem vague to rational minds. Logically, the theory of the "invisible hand" should long since have been forgotten, except perhaps by those who are interested in the history—or indeed the prehistory—of economics. But this is not what happened. Adam Smith's anthropomorphic intuition has withstood the test of time and the scorn of critics, and its fascination is much greater today than it was two hundred and fifty years ago.

Its longevity can primarily be explained by the dismal failure of the Soviet model, which had made a strong case for the "scientific" nature of its socialism. The model was designed to demonstrate that only government could streamline production and distribution. Instead, it proved the opposite, that the more centralized an economy became, the more absurd its implementation; even as it claimed to manage resources, it produced greater shortages.

As a result, it was "scientific socialism" that was relegated to the dustbin of history, while the "invisible hand" reemerged, and was seen as so credible and so legitimate that conservative activists considered it the founding principle of their ideology. Even the mysterious and somewhat irrational nature of the idea was appealing; many have seen it as having a spiritual dimension, as God sanctioning capitalism against the "atheist" intervention.

*

The precepts of Adam Smith shape our world today much more so than they did in the past. And not simply in terms of the role of the State in economic affairs: the belief in the "invisible hand" has had consequences in many other areas.

It is not difficult to understand that those who distrust their own government are even more mistrustful of international organizations—the same mindset is at work. Someone who does not want government to intervene in the economic affairs of the nation will certainly not want some supranational authority issuing directives. Anyone who decides that there is "too much government" in their country will be suspicious of any organization that smacks of a "global government," such as the United Nations; or even a "regional government," such as the European Parliament that sits in Brussels.

In the same way, these people are instinctively suspicious of Cassandras who predict global catastrophes and call for a solidarity that transcends national boundaries. While I do not wish to dwell on the debate around climate change, it seems appropriate to point out that conflicting reactions to it proceed from a similar dichotomy. Those hostile to global governance will tend to espouse arguments that question the reality of global warming and human responsibility for such changes. Conversely, those who trust international bodies will tend to believe the most catastrophic predictions.

Having emphasized the resilience and extraordinary longevity of the doctrine espoused by Adam Smith, I feel I should add that its ability to triumph over Marxism does not make it an adequate response to the challenges of the world today.

The fact that socialist interventionism was a fallacious ideology does not necessarily mean that the "invisible hand" is the providential solution to all our present and future ills. When it comes to the environment, for example, is it really conceivable that if everyone acts according to their own self-interest, it will be beneficial for the country as a whole, for the planet as a whole? The answer, obviously, is no; yet there are some—especially in the United States—who nonetheless seem to believe it.

What about the relationships between countries? Is it enough for each to act according to its own self-interest, its own ambitions, to ensure that humanity will move forward towards peace and prosperity? Again, the answer is no. But those citizens wary of the government "interfering" in their business are even more wary of anything that resembles global or supranational governance.

If I have laid particular stress on these facts, it is because I find it disconcerting that, in a globalized world, where images, tools, ideas, and even viruses and illnesses can spread at the speed of light, the prevailing ideology is one based on the sacred self-interest of individuals and their "tribes"—nations, ethnic groups, and communities of every kind.

It is easy to chart the historical course that has led to such attitudes. But it is difficult not to be concerned by our excessive confidence in the "algebraic sum" of our self-interests. Plainly, there has been a drift towards the irrational, to a kind of magical thinking, that reveals a profound feeling of helplessness when faced with the complexities of the world. Unable to come up with adequate solutions, we allow ourselves to believe that the solutions will come of themselves, by some miracle, and that it is enough to have faith in the "invisible hand" of Heaven, or of fate.

This, I fear, does not bode well for the decades ahead.

2

Another disquieting facet of our times, one that is based on the same worldview, is the acceptance of inequalities, however stark.

It is true that few people today consider effective equality between all human beings to be an achievable goal. Yet until now the concept of equality, however misused, was seen as a symbolic moral reference; certainly no one dared to openly champion inequality. Though we accepted inequality as inevitable, no one thought to applaud it. One might make a similar observation about unemployment: it has been some time since anyone truly believed in full employment, but, in the past, stock markets around the world did not frantically buy stocks in those companies engaged in massive layoffs.

This is what has changed with the new zeitgeist. Even in France, my adopted country, although people still invoke the principle of equality, they also contemplate outrageous wealth with fascination rather than with horror; and if they are still shocked by the salaries of certain business leaders, they are blasé when it comes to footballers, actors, or pop stars. This attitude is even more pronounced in countries like Russia or China, where a veneer of egalitarianism has long served as a cover for injustice and tyranny.

Meanwhile, when the media publish one of their frequent rankings of the greatest private fortunes in the world as compared to the wealth of the rest of mankind, it no longer provokes outrage. No one these days expects an uprising among the "wretched of the earth," and it would be terrifying if the workers were to rise from their slumber and at last end the age of cant, as in the lyrics of the "Internationale." Such an uprising could only lead to a bloodbath, to an orgy of destruction. Not something to be hoped for by those who still cherish the ideals of progress, freedom, decency, or even equality itself. If inequality is disturbing today, it is not because it causes revolutions around the world, but because the notion of equality, which served as a moral compass, has faded, and this has contributed to the disintegration of the social fabric in every country, and in humanity in general.

This observation seems obvious to anyone who follows the workings of the world, but it is difficult to substantiate with concrete evidence. How can one prove that, in an age where extreme wealth fires the imagination, it is inevitable that corruption will spread through the ruling classes and infect society as a whole? That when the self-interest of individuals and groups is considered acceptable, legitimate, or even the work of providence, the solidarity between the different parts of a population is stretched to breaking point? That seeing the "rich and famous" as role models, even if they are crooks, means discrediting the entire value system?

In his fable *The Grasshopper and the Ant*, La Fontaine illustrated the moral system of his time, one that seemed universal and enduring: that the diligent, daily hard work of the ant was a moral value that her neighbour the grasshopper should have embraced, instead of singing "all summer long."

In La Fontaine's fable, the ant has the starring role. The reader approves of her industriousness, her tireless work throughout the year, and laughs as she mocks: "You were singing? How entrancing! Well then, missy, go try dancing!" The grasshopper, on the other hand, feels awkward and embarrassed at having to beg for food. Today, the situation is reversed. Now, it is the ants who are mocked and scorned. Young people who have watched their parents slave all their lives, without ever being financially comfortable, let alone rich or famous, feel pity rather than respect. They are not encouraged to follow their parents' example. On the contrary, they feel encouraged to break away, to strive for their fifteen minutes of fame, to emulate those who "made it," those who managed to "get rich," even if this means racketeering or sordid dealings.

It is impossible to overstate how much the reversal of values can change a society; when people begin to admire what used to be considered reprehensible and despise what was considered exemplary. It hardly needs explaining that a neighbourhood in which drug dealers are more respected than teachers is a breeding ground for social decay. And when a society prizes activities that are lucrative over those that are socially useful, the disastrous consequences are impossible to control. It influences the behaviour of citizens in every sphere …

*

Like many of those involved with art or literature, I identify with both the ant and the grasshopper, and I would be wary of pronouncing on the relative merits of their activities. My chief concern, once again, is witnessing those elements that fragment human society prevailing over those that bring us together.

In the first pages of this book, I evoked the unsettling paradox of a world in which progress in science, technology, and economic development have continued, but that in other crucial areas, particularly those concerning the relationship between its various human communities, is treading water and perhaps even slipping backwards.

In considering the effects of the invisible hand theory on economic and social policies, we find ourselves at the very heart of this paradox. On the one hand, the theory has unleashed energy, boosted trade, and accelerated innovation; on the other, in denigrating the regulatory role of government and glorifying excessive wealth, it has undermined the very idea of community, and weakened the bonds between citizens.

The downside is not simply unquestionable, it has had grave consequences, even if they are difficult to pinpoint. How does one put a value on the loss of public-spiritedness? How does one measure the strengthening or weakening of ties between various communities within a population? How does one demonstrate the link between the mistrust of government and the rise of communitarianism, violence, and corruption? We are dealing with things that are elusive and unquantifiable; it would serve no purpose to set out facts and figures.

My feeling, however, is that the drift humanity is experiencing today is linked to the change in attitudes towards the role of government, as fostered by the conservative revolutions.

To be more explicit, I shall begin by asking: What is the glue that binds human societies together? What is it that makes individuals or groups want to live together, to be part of a community, a nation? This is not a rhetorical question; it is something about which I am genuinely curious, and about which I have no fixed opinion. There are many factors that can bind the citizens of a country: the sense of a common future; a common ancestry; common values; even a common enemy ... The list is not exhaustive, and it changes over time.

One characteristic of this century is that there are

fewer and fewer commonalities. I almost added, "especially in pluralistic countries." But the distinction is superfluous. All societies are pluralistic, though some more readily admit it. And, so, all of them have difficulties in creating strong bonds between individuals, between families and communities whose lives, traditions, and histories are different.

The traditional formulas that have for many centuries formed nations are no longer of much use. If people have no common ancestors, they cannot invent them. If there is no "national narrative" accepted by everyone, one cannot be imposed. Even common values no longer act as "glue." We wish they would, we behave as though they do, but more often than not this is merely a self-indulgent fiction rather than a reflection of reality.

And all around the world people find themselves helpless, powerless, holding forth about integration, about inclusiveness, about the virtues of diversity, even as the ties that bind them are fraying; and they resort to their innate ties, those that are more visible and more visceral, those that do not require real freedom of choice. Everyone simply follows their own natural bent, in keeping with the spirit of the times.

There are so many examples I could cite. I shall simply mention racial tensions in the United States. One might think that, after the advances in civil rights, and especially after the powerful symbol represented by the election of Barack Obama as president, these tensions would have subsided. Instead, the opposite has happened, relations have rather soured.

Obviously Anglo-Saxon, Latinx, and African-American citizens do not share common ancestors. But one might hope that they recognize a similar vision of their country, and a common destiny. But it is clear that things are going in the opposite direction.

Could it have been otherwise? Is it naive to think that racial tensions might have been less severe if rampant inequality had not been given free rein? If Reagan had not declared war on social security and the fictional welfare queen?

The way I have phrased this question betrays my personal conviction. I am one of those who think that if we invest wisely in social harmony, we can reduce tensions between the different groups within a nation. I am even tempted to repeat what I said earlier about Mandela and his approach to addressing racial tensions in his country: it so happens that magnanimity is the lesser evil; and it happens that a good deed can also be a good deal.

Nevertheless, in an effort to remain objective I feel I should say that history has not yet decided. Neither on the thorny issue of race relations in South Africa or the United States; nor on the broader and much older issue of the role that government should or should not play in the redistribution of wealth. I am not unmoved by the arguments of those who rail against bureaucracy and red tape or the increasing burden of taxes and tariffs. However, it seems to me that government plays a subtle, abstract, yet irreplaceable role. In a thousand different ways, government helps to build relationships, reinforces a sense of belonging; when it is systematically disparaged, it can no longer fulfil this role.

As a result, while it is legitimate to question whether government, as Reagan said, can sometimes be "the problem," it is equally legitimate to ask whether the lack of government does not sometimes pose a much more serious problem.

3

While the primary effect of the conservative revolutions has been to challenge the role of the interventionist state, a secondary effect, as I briefly mentioned earlier, has been the rise of identity politics. It seems to me that the combined effects of these two factors broadly explain the drift that humanity has experienced in this century.

As we have already seen, the impact of the former is difficult to define. The same cannot be said about the latter, whose toxic effects are visible to the naked eye. Identity politics have poisoned the atmosphere of the planet as a whole, along with each of its individual societies. But, although we are routinely confronted by the violence that, in practice, results, the underlying theory somehow "clouds the issue," since it speaks of solidarity, fraternity, of remedying injustices, and it can be difficult to recognize the pernicious effects beyond these rallying cries.

This is what I was alluding to when I talked about the things that truly bind human societies, as opposed to those which are supposed to, but do not. For example, religion is routinely mentioned in discussions about identity politics, and is fearsomely effective in instilling a sense of "us" and "them" among co-religionists. Yet, when studied closely, it is rarely a factor in cohesion. Even among the faithful. This is particularly true when it comes to the great global religions. The more these have spread, conquered, and converted, the less capable they have proven to be at forging strong political links among their followers. At best, they promote certain cultural affinities. The most powerful societal bonds seem to be the preserve of small communities, which, feeling their vulnerability, experience the need to join forces, something that often affords them an influence at odds with their demographic numbers.

How often have we heard that certain communities play a major role "despite being a minority"? It might be more accurate to say that they have influence "because they are a minority." As the fourteenth-century historian Ibn Khaldun noted, "clannishness" comes more easily to small groups; it strengthens their cohesion and can give them a decisive advantage in their dealings with others. One of the best-known cases today is that of the Alawites in Syria, to which the Assad family belong. In the 1960s Alawite military officers succeeded in taking control of the army, and by 1970 had seized political power, which they have retained ever since. A similar phenomenon occurred in Iraq with the Sunni Arab clan of which Saddam Hussein was a member; it required an all-out invasion by US troops to force them to loosen their grip.

Such powerful cohesion can exist only within a small community. It is unimaginable in a larger group, and impossible in the vast "areas of civilization" spanned by major global religions like Christianity, Islam, or Buddhism, which together make up half the world's population, and whose adherents represent a majority in many countries.

As a result of their remarkable expansion, these three religions have taken root in societies that are marked by a wide disparity of languages, cultural traditions, political and family structures; societies that are sometimes riven by territorial disputes, conflicts of interest, or even simply a vague antipathy whose origins are lost in the mists of time; societies in which conflicts are not resolved, but rekindled under the banner of religion.

One example seems to me to be particularly telling. In 1947, the British authorities decided to grant independence to the Indian subcontinent, but in doing so they divided it into two states: to the Hindus, they gave India; to the Muslims, Pakistan.

For the former, things did not go too badly. Although there are more than a billion adherents to Hinduism, it is essentially the religion of a single country, and, as a result, facilitates a relative national cohesion. I personally believe that India would have developed more rapidly and more smoothly if it hadn't been for this harrowing and traumatic partition, since the large Muslim population, traditionally hostile to the caste system, would probably have shaken up some of the secular barriers. I will not try to demonstrate this, it is simply a personal intuition ... What we know for certain—and this is not a personal intuition but rather proven fact—is that, for the Muslims of the subcontinent, partition was a terrible tragedy.

The idea behind partition was that the nations of either side of the divide would be masters of their own destiny, stimulated to outperform their neighbour and to lead by example. The founding fathers of Pakistan, many of them valiant men, were convinced that Islam would "cement" this new nation, which brought together peoples who had different languages and social traditions, but who shared a common faith.

The largest demographic were the Bengalis, who lived in what was then East Pakistan, and who felt abandoned by the Punjabi-dominated central government based in West Pakistan. These tensions came to a head in November 1970, when Bengal was hit by a devastating tropical cyclone, the deadliest ever recorded. At least 250,000 people died; perhaps as many as half a million.

Leaders in the eastern province accused the central government of "callous and utter indifference" in its failure to help victims, civil unrest turned to open rebellion, and within months East Pakistan unilaterally declared its independence as the People's Republic of Bangladesh. The Pakistani government attempted to oppose this move by force, but were defeated when the Indian Army intervened, and were forced to accept the secession.

I visited the new state shortly after its foundation. The damage from the cyclone was still visible, although it was difficult to tell the difference between the hardships caused by the disaster and those due to chronic poverty. Whole families were living in large concrete pipes, and even they were better off than those who were forced to live on the roadside, with no shelter whatsoever.

The most harrowing images I saw while I was there were not these, however, but images of the terrible plight of the Bihari people. The Biharis—a Muslim ethnic minority who had immigrated from the Indian province that shares their name—had been in favour of preserving a united Pakistan and had sided with the central government against the separatists. Consequently, after independence they were treated as enemies of the new nation. They were the poorest of the poor, all their possessions were confiscated, and they were locked away in empty, insalubrious buildings, pending a decision about their fate.

I said "locked away," but this was not quite the case— the armed guards stationed at the doors were there to prevent the "patriots" outside from persecuting the "traitors," who, for their part, made no attempt to venture out.

I have often thought about the terrible fate suffered by the Biharis, though many other peoples have since joined the list of the defeated and the persecuted—particularly the Rohingyas, in neighbouring Myanmar. In a world where the seething issue of identity prevails, everyone is necessarily a traitor in the eyes of someone, and sometimes in the eyes of everyone. Every member of a minority, every migrant, every citizen of the world, every person with dual nationality is potentially a "traitor" ...

*

In hindsight, the example of Pakistan prompts other, more unsettling observations.

Firstly, once you accept the logic of "partition," it triggers an infinite loop of potential fragmentation. First, Muslims are separated from Hindus; then Bengalis from Punjabis. But within each of the states where these people are the majority, there are other peoples who then fear being crushed, persecuted, perhaps even annihilated; should they, too, be given their own country?

"However small a fish, there is always a smaller fish," a disillusioned historian once said to me. And it is true that, once one accepts partition as an effective solution, the "salami-slicing" can go on indefinitely ...

Secondly, when a particular people become the majority in a country, they do not become more tolerant, they become paradoxically less so. I say "paradoxically" because, in theory, people choose to be among their "own kind" so that they do not have to fear intrusions by a rival group; by this logic, those in the majority should feel more secure, and hence more magnanimous. Sadly, that is not what happens in practice. In fact, the reverse is true: it is only when minorities have a significant influence and their opinions are reflected in public debate that political regimes seek to structure their society in a way that that is tolerant and just. When minorities lose this influence, when only the opinion of the majority can be heard, countries descend into populism and political parties vie to outdo each other.

Every country that creates a communitarian system comes to experience this drift, but in Pakistan it has reached a horrifying apogee, a visceral surge of intolerance rarely seen elsewhere. In Pakistan, all minorities are persecuted and humiliated, and anyone who seeks to defend those minorities or to introduce a modicum of sanity and serenity to public life suffers the same fate. This is a tragedy for the nation as a whole, regardless of affiliation.

Homogeneity is a costly and cruel chimera. People pay dearly in their efforts to attain it, and if they succeed, they pay more dearly still.

My third observation is based on the first two, and extrapolates from them somewhat. I wonder whether the drift of humankind that we are seeing today is not the result of the bad habit, first adopted in the early nineteenth century, of breaking up great empires in which many people rubbed shoulders in order to create nations where these people could live separately.

Sometimes I even wonder whether the theory of empire as a "prison of peoples" who must be liberated so that they can live "amongst themselves," with their own government and their own borders, has not been the deadliest of modern times.

I am thinking particularly about the fate of two large multiethnic states that were dismantled after the First World War: the Austro-Hungarian Empire, whose breakup resulted in tens of millions of victims and fostered the rise of some of the worst tyrannies of the modern age; and the dismantling of the Ottoman Empire, a process that continues to this day, and has cast a pall of terror and regression over all humanity.

I am certainly not suggesting that I feel a nostalgia for these empires; I do not dream of seeing them restored. Not the empire of the Habsburgs nor the Tsars, still less that of the Sultans. What I do regret is the disappearance of a particular mindset that existed in the time of empires, one that considered it normal and acceptable for peoples to be part of a single political entity without necessarily sharing the same religion, the same language, or even the same history. I have never accepted the idea that peoples with different languages or different religions would be better off living independently of each other. I will never accept the notion that ethnicity, religion, or race are legitimate foundations on which to build nations.

How many abject failures, how many massacres, how much "ethnic cleansing" must we endure before this barbaric approach to the issue of identity ceases to be considered normal, realistic, and "consistent with human nature"?

4

Over the course of the preceding chapters, I have talked about my regrets, my remorse, and my nostalgia or my melancholy. In looking back over one's life and taking stock, such notions necessarily come to mind, and one can but acknowledge them, even if they seem inadequate, inappropriate, or even utterly irrational. How often have I lamented the disappearance of an "earthly paradise" I never knew? How often have I felt shame, or even a twinge of guilt for things that happened before I was born? As though, in setting down the moral legacy of my forefathers, I was also obliged to shoulder the blame for their illusions, their disillusions, and their mistakes.

It is in order to avoid this constant failing that I have grown accustomed to referring to all the tragedies that have affected my era and my own life by a single, anodyne word, *sorrow*—sometimes *sorrows*, plural—to connect this nebulous feeling to individual memories.

All my sorrows follow the same path, that of a great hope thwarted, betrayed, distorted, or destroyed. Successive childhood sorrows for the loss of the twin paradises of my mother and my father. Sorrow for all the peoples of the Levant—without exception—all those I am supposed to think of as "other" and all those I am expected to think of as "my own," who are drowning in a mire and hurling abuse at one another. Recurring sorrows for those Arab societies that, once or twice in a generation, try to take wing, soar for a moment, fall and tumble to earth like hawks with broken wings. Sorrow for the magnanimous ideals that stirred my youth, and which, in my twilight years, have been misused and discredited: universality, the rising curve of history, the harmonious flowering of cultures, the convergence of values, and the equal dignity of all human beings.

One of my great sorrows these days concerns Europe. Whenever I raise the subject, people tell me that I am too demanding, that I should bear in mind what the continent was like for countless centuries and until very recently: a battlefield between unfettered nationalisms and a proving ground for the most terrible atrocities ... Surely that dark page in history has been turned forever? These days, we cross the French–German border without even realizing it, as though we were in the same country, as if the bloody battles for Alsace-Lorraine had never happened. When in Berlin, we move between East and West oblivious to the line that marks where the wall once stood. Where else in the world has experienced such things? Certainly not the region where I was born. The Levant has followed a very different path, one that has turned many of the regions and cities I visited in my youth into no-go areas.

So I am not attempting to disparage the remarkable progress made by Europe since the end of World War II; I commend it with all my heart. But I cannot deny that, these days, I feel a certain disillusionment. Because I expected more from my adoptive continent: I expected it to provide a moral compass for all humanity, one that might prevent it from straying, from fragmenting into tribes, communities, factions, and clans.

When I consider the upheavals of this century, I sometimes regret that there is no political and moral authority to which our contemporaries can turn with confidence and hope; one that cherishes universal values and has the power to influence the course of history. And when I survey the world and tentatively wonder who might take on such a task, it seems to me that only Europe could do so, if it gave itself the means.

Why Europe? I grant that it is not an "obvious candidate." Logically, the role should fall to the United States of America, which has long shown the will to exercise global leadership, and has the necessary qualifications. From the outset, the principles upon which the United States was built have expressed a genuine concern for universal values, and its ethnic makeup reflects the broad diversity of the world—imperfectly, perhaps, but more so than any other major country. Above all, in the twentieth century the United States has risen to become the foremost world power in every sphere: industrial production, military force, scientific research, political and intellectual influence, etc. Having won three major global wars—the First and Second World Wars, and the Cold War—they have earned a primacy among nations that no one can seriously challenge. Logically, they should long ago have become the beacon of reference for all humanity. But they have failed to live up to this responsibility.

The most surprising thing is that their failure, which now seems self-evident, cannot be blamed on a loss of power—which, as I write, remains formidable—nor on the actions of their enemies, but on the inability of successive leaders to persuasively accept the supremacy they have acquired.

*

Donald Trump's numerous detractors like to believe that the crumbling moral stature of their country dates from his presidency. As I see it, the turning point came much earlier, as the Cold War was ending. At the time, the United States found itself in a position that no other country on earth has been able to claim since the dawn of history, as the only global superpower. They could unilaterally have laid the foundations of a new world order; no one seriously questioned their supremacy.

Mikhail Gorbachev, the last leader of the Soviet Union, had resolved to commit his country to a path of economic and political liberalization, and seemed prepared to give up the vast Eastern European empire carved out by Stalin after the Second World War. Faced with an unexpected situation, one that exceeded its wildest hopes, the United States had a choice: either it could support Gorbachev's plan, offer him the economic and political support he needed to facilitate the difficult and courageous transition on which he had embarked; or it could exploit the weakness of the rival superpower in order to crush it.

For the United States, this was a thorny dilemma. It had spent forty years waging proxy wars around the globe against a formidable adversary whose military arsenal represented a lethal threat. Now that the Soviet Union was down, should the USA help it get back on its feet? Or take advantage of the situation to rid itself of a bitter rival once and for all? The latter option seemed the most pragmatic, and is the one they adopted. The United States did nothing to save Gorbachev, the Soviet Union was allowed to collapse and was then dismembered. Several of its former republics were integrated into NATO, despite vehement protests from Moscow.

In Washington, a few lone voices spoke up to say that this was a mistake. The most notable of these was George F. Kennan, a widely respected elder statesman, who at the time was almost a living legend. It was he who, in the 1940s, had warned America not to place too much trust in its Soviet ally, that a long and bitter clash would take place between the two world powers; it was he who first stressed the need for a policy of "containment" to prevent the Soviet Union from expanding—militarily, politically, ideologically. Kennan was universally acknowledged as having played a decisive role in winning the Cold War, culminating in the fall of the Berlin Wall in 1989. He was celebrated as one of the chief architects of the strategy, and a model of clear-sightedness and determination.

Now that the victory he had fought to achieve had been won, Kennan's essential message to his countrymen, and especially to those policymakers who consulted him, might be summed up: *Let us not forget why we fought! We wanted democracy to triumph over dictatorship, and we have succeeded. We must now draw the necessary conclusions. We cannot continue to treat former enemies as though they will be enemies forever!* What exemplified the veteran diplomat was that his passionate loathing for the Soviet system was matched by a deep love for the Russian people, their culture, and their literature—particularly Chekhov.

But although he insisted over and over that humiliating the Russians would merely encourage the rise of nationalist and militarist movements, and slow any progress towards democracy, no one was prepared to listen. As happens all too often, sadly, in moments of triumph, the magnanimity Kennan advocated was perceived as weakness and naivety. The view that prevailed was that the United States should press its advantage, without hesitation, and not allow itself to be mollified by moral scruples or intellectual qualms. In 1997, when President Clinton asked one of his advisors whether he should have listened to Kennan's warnings, he was told that the veteran diplomat was mistaken, that the Russians would eventually accept everything the United States imposed, because they had no choice.

It would be futile to cast the first stone at this or that American president or one of his advisors. Because the task they were faced with as they emerged from the Cold War was difficult and delicate. They could not simply take on an existing role, they had to fashion a role out of whole cloth, and to do so in a political landscape unlike anything the world had seen. I feel it is important to underscore this point, which seems to me essential in understanding how the great nation of America came to drift, and dragged all humanity in its wake.

The United States had long dreamed of playing a "paternal" role towards the rest of the world, guiding certain countries, admonishing others—and indeed, in the aftermath of both World Wars, the United States did play such a role. After the Great War the United States worked to rebuild a shattered Europe through the Marshall Plan, and after the Second World War, it helped transform Japan into a peaceful democracy.

But their justification for such interventions was that they helped to defeat Soviet Communism. The very concept of a global strategy not focused on fighting an enemy seemed absurd. The idea that all the countries of the world might become allies or dependents flies in the face of political practice since time immemorial. It is only in the face of some threat, some enemy, that countries mobilize, that they sharpen their swords, and forge alliances. Sadly, all too often a foreign threat becomes a polestar without which we nations no longer know where we are headed, what we are doing, or even who we are. I am not among those who think that this will always be true, but the predisposition has been so deep-rooted for so long that we will have to be highly inventive and very daring if we are to find a different way of seeing the world. Of seeing others and ourselves.

It was precisely this daring and inventiveness that the leaders of the United States needed at the end of the Cold War. How should a superpower act now it no longer had a rival? How should it treat its former enemies? Should it help them redevelop and recover? And what of its former allies? Should it continue to treat them as friends, or should it simply see them as commercial rivals? And what of the rest of the world? Should the United States play the role of "global policeman" or should it allow the countless nations, tribes, and factions around the world to clash at will? Each of these approaches came with benefits, risks, and uncertainties.

With hindsight, it is clear that the United States failed the difficult test set by history. In the three decades that followed their triumph and their coronation, they proved unable to establish a new world order, to build a role as a parental power, or indeed to sustain their moral credibility, which is probably lower today than at any time in the last century. Their former adversaries have once more become adversaries, but their former allies no longer truly feel like allies.

This moral collapse did not occur overnight; it is the culmination of a long series of blunders, gaffes, setbacks, and missteps, under the aegis of a series of presidents whose policies were often poles apart.

At times the United States has been fanatically interventionist, as during the 2003 Iraq War; they have tried to bring down regimes, restructure countries, and re-order whole regions according to their own worldview.

At other times, weary of the heavy responsibility they had rashly taken upon themselves, American leaders have reversed this policy, pledging not to intervene, not to send troops, but to instead allow local factions to massacre each other. The latter policy reached its apogee in September 2013; despite issuing an unequivocal warning to Syria that the use of chemical weapons constituted a red line that would lead to forceful military intervention, President Obama eventually decided that it was not in his best interests to intervene.

Unfortunately, many aggressors around the world may have interpreted this climbdown as a licence to act with impunity.

I have cited three or four incidents here; I could cite countless others. Like my contemporaries, I have watched in recent decades as the United States has strutted across the world stage with a thousand different faces. We have seen a magnanimous America and a mean-minded America, an arrogant America and a timorous America. In September 2001, we saw an America that was wounded and grieving, and longed to comfort it, to reassure America that we cherished the values it represented and everything it had given to the world. Two years later, during the Iraq War, we witnessed a vicious, cynical, destructive, intolerable America.

To be fair, I should add that the same behaviour on the part of any other country would have aroused little outrage—but that is not the issue. This is not about deciding whether, faced with a particular crisis, the actions of Washington were better or worse than those of Berlin, Paris, Moscow, or Beijing. It is about determining whether the United States is worthy of assuming the role of arbiter or tutelary power with regard to other nations. And the answer to that, sadly, is a resounding *No*. America's failings have been obvious, they have only continued to increase, and they now seem all but irreparable.

In this delicate phase of human history, people feel the need for a "captain" who cares about the fate of the ship, rather than simply his own. It would have been simultaneously ludicrous and grotesque if, seeing people running for the lifeboats, the captain of the *Titanic* had yelled into his loudhailer, "Stand back! Me first!"

5

Would Europe have been better able than the USA to assume this "parental" role? To lay the foundations of a new world order that reflected new realities, to set rules and guidelines, and to ensure that the rest of the world respected them?

We shall never know, because the old world never acquired the necessary resources. But I believe, at the very least, that it could have been an able "first mate," loyally supporting a hotheaded America while tempering its wilder moments.

Why Europe? For a number of reasons, none of which is in itself decisive but which, taken together, indicate that it was uniquely predisposed to take on this historic responsibility.

Firstly, Europe was the birthplace of the industrial revolution and the civilization that accompanied it, and therefore, in a sense, the "furnace" in which modern humanity was forged. It is no insult to the Levant, the cradle of the most ancient civilizations, to acknowledge that in the past three centuries everything of consequence—ideas, tools, weapons, a whole way of life—has come from Europe.

I mention "my" Levant only by way of example. European civilization became a benchmark not simply for us, but for the whole world. It is understandable that people should feel irritated by such hegemony, and entirely reasonable to assume that it will not last forever; but it is impossible to deny that Europe's is the civilization by which all others are judged, given that *its* science has become global science, *its* technology has become global technology, *its* philosophy has become global philosophy, its view of economics has no credible rivals, and anything that has not been touched by its grace—for better or for worse—has become peripheral, archaic, invisible, and almost nonexistent.

The hegemony I have described belongs to the Western world as a whole, to the United States at least as much as Europe. But when it comes to assuming a "parental" role vis-à-vis the rest of the world, Europe has certain qualities that its "daughter" across the Atlantic—however energetic and powerful—sorely lacks.

One of the great advantages of the old world is that history has taught its people many, often painful, lessons. Granted, the nations of Europe conquered every corner of the globe and dominated it for centuries, but in time they learned the limits of such dominance, and this made them wiser, more responsible, and sometimes, it must be admitted, more timid.

For most Europeans, the arrogance of colonialism has given way to a more prudent, more respectful attitude towards others.

*

Equally important to me are the lessons that Europe has learned from its own internal rifts. In striving to overcome them, it set about writing a crucial page in human history.

After the Second World War, the engineers of the European project realized that it was essential to rebuild the continent on very different foundations, to encourage different peoples to set aside ancient conflicts and live together as different branches of a single nation.

The idea was hardly a new one; it has been formulated by eminent writers down the centuries, including Erasmus and Victor Hugo, to name but two. But today, there are specific factors that give the European project a particular universal significance.

Like Europe, the rest of the world in which we live is divided into independent countries, each with its own history, its own national narrative, languages, beliefs, cultural references, and often its own age-old conflicts with its neighbours.

Whether or not they realize it, all countries, large or small, rich or poor, would benefit by transcending old enmities and ensuring a powerful influence in the world by integrating into larger bodies in which all nations, all languages, and all cultures could preserve their existence and their dignity.

This presupposes that there exists a model from which these various countries could learn. A "pilot project" that is already underway, and can offer concrete examples of how to break with old habits and live together in peace. Only the European project could offer such a model, since it aspired to bring together countries that had until then waged war on each other throughout history, and were now striving to build a common future.

If the old world had succeeded in building its own United States, it could have proven that such a future is not merely a utopia or a chimera, but genuinely feasible.

Granted, to truly serve as a reference model, the European Union would have had to become a federal state with all the attributes of a global power, in political and military as well as economic terms. But it did not have the necessary will. Doubtless the peoples of Europe had little appetite for such a role. And doubtless the leaders of the various countries were reluctant to shed the fig leaf of sovereignty.

The tragedy for Europe is that, in this ruthless world of ours, to choose not to become a major power means that you can be pushed around and held to ransom. Rather than becoming a respected arbiter, you become a potential victim, and a future hostage.

*

Hence the frustration I feel today when I think about the fate of my adoptive continent. Of course, the European Union was established, it has grown, and it represents a vast improvement on what once existed. But it is a fragile, unfinished, hybrid structure, and one that is now being violently shaken.

I call it "hybrid" because those who founded the European Union were unable to choose between the two paths open to them: a fully-fledged, irrevocable union like the United States of America or a simple free-trade area. They wanted to believe that this decision could be made at a later date—but it cannot. A decision that could be made between six or nine countries becomes impossible when the number of countries rises to twenty-seven or twenty-eight. Especially if the decision must be unanimous, as is now the case for all the fundamental decisions of the EU.

Truth be told, the EU has been guilty of an excess of democracy, in giving each country a veto and thus preventing any progress towards a genuine union; and simultaneously a lack of democracy, in deciding to entrust power to the Brussels commissioners appointed by each country, rather than to a European government directly elected by EU citizens.

People with a long experience of democracy cannot easily accept leaders who have not been elected by popular vote.

There are a thousand things one might say about this European experiment that was, to my mind, one of the most promising in human history, and is now beginning to unravel before our eyes. As I have previously said, it is one of the greatest sorrows of our time. Even if I were to ignore the other events around the world and focus only on the slow crumbling of the European dream, I would still feel minded to call it a shipwreck ...

6

Perhaps I have leaned too heavily on the naval metaphor in suggesting that without a steadfast "captain" at the helm, the "ship" of mankind is bound to sink. The obliteration of the human race has been predicted a thousand times, but we are still here, more prosperous, more inventive, more ambitious than ever. In spite of all our destructive impulses and all our follies. Is this a sign that I should finally accept that down the centuries an "invisible hand" has indeed been preserving us from annihilation?

While such a theory goes against my vision of the world, I cannot simply dismiss it. Because I must admit this vision contains some grain of truth. Like all those who lived through the Cold War, for decades I lived in fear of the nuclear holocaust that we were told was inevitable. How many times did we hear that, through the actions of some madman or a series of mistakes, the thousands of warheads amassed by the global superpowers would inevitably lead to a world war that would utterly destroy our civilization? Only a fool, we were told, would believe that the brinkmanship between the two global powers could end without an apocalyptic conflagration.

And yet, that is precisely what happened. On the day that one superpower gained an absolute advantage, the losing power accepted defeat without a single missile being launched. We emerged from the minefield unscathed, as though guided—yes—by an invisible hand. Would it really be absurd to hope that, when faced with the perils that lie ahead, we can once again trust to providence?

I have long wanted to accept this reassuring vision of history; even now, despite my concerns, some part of me still clings to it. Not because I blindly trust in the wisdom of mankind, but for a very different reason, one that relates to the peculiarities of our era and the laws that govern its transformation.

The complex phenomenon we call "globalization," by the very nature of the technologies on which it relies, has created a powerful and profound momentum pushing the different sectors of humanity closer to one another. This enforced closeness, whether physical or virtual, has fostered both affinities and antagonisms. To my mind, one of the major issues of our time is to know which of the two will eventually prevail. Will we see identity-related tensions diminish and disappear? Or will they grow steadily worse, causing greater fragmentation and division?

In looking at events around the world, we are particularly struck by movements fuelled by division and hatred. Because they are undeniably compelling; but also because they are more dramatic, more forceful, more spectacular than those movements stemming from convergence and affinity, which are more subtle, more unobtrusive, and all too often underestimated. Yet the latter kind of movement has historically been dynamic and forceful, with effects that can be observed in all human societies.

I would go so far as to say that never before have birds of a feather more clearly flocked together. Try as societies might to hate each other, to fight with each other, they cannot help but imitate each other. Wherever they find themselves, they have the same tools, they have access to the same information and the same images, they are constantly acquiring common behaviours and common references.

Where once we instinctively tended to mimic the gestures of our parents and our grandparents, today we tend to instinctively imitate the behaviour of our contemporaries. This is not something to which we readily admit. We staunchly maintain the myth that behaviour is transmitted "vertically," from one generation to the next, in families, in clans, in nations, and in religious communities, whereas in fact it is transmitted "horizontally," among contemporaries, whether or not they know each other, whether they love or hate each other.

I have to confess that this fact has often comforted me in times of distress. When I looked around and saw the stark rise of identity-related tensions and outbursts of hatred, I comforted myself with the thought that they were merely rearguard actions, the convulsive death throes of a world that was already disappearing, already obsolete, already sinking, and was clinging desperately to the practices and prejudices of the past.

*

What concerned me slightly, however, and now concerns me rather more, is that while this unifying momentum affects all our contemporaries unconsciously, it is not something that is consciously considered by anyone. In a sense one might say that this powerful subterranean force is an "orphan," in that, while our contemporaries are being moulded and shaped by the unifying wave created by technological advances, they continue to cling to dogmas that persist in glorifying the individual.

With each passing day our contemporaries are becoming ever more alike, despite their conflicts and their mutual antipathies. This paradox seems less reassuring if phrased differently: this steady progress towards universality has been accompanied by a gradual weakening of the movements and ideologies that advocate that very universality.

A powerful and often aggressive assertion of identity has always formed a crucial part of the discourse of those powers currently in the ascendant, by which I mean those conservative revolutions. This can be seen everywhere, from Africa to Europe, in Arab countries and in Israel, in India and in the United States.

The current behaviour of some traditionally left-wing organizations is equally unsettling: where once they raised the banner of humanism and universalism, they now champion identity politics, setting themselves up as spokespersons for various ethnic, community, or sectional minorities as though, having given up trying to build a project for society as a whole, they hope to regain a majority by forming a collation of resentments.

There is nothing ignoble or wrong in this, especially since the claims of these oppressed minorities are often morally justified. But when a movement bases its strategy on divisions, it is inevitably contributing to fragmentation and division.

This shift in the perspective and language of the advocates of progressivism is the result of a phenomenon that I have already mentioned, namely the shift of the intellectual "balance of power" in the world, marked by the inexorable rise of conservative forces who now set the terms of the debate. The losers have been forced to give up their own "thinking tools" and adopt those of the winners, which they then try to turn to their advantage. The ideologies that promoted universality have been so discredited in recent decades that any and all specific local characteristics have somehow been legitimized.

The fault lies primarily with the mistakes made by Marxism, but it is not merely Marxism that has suffered the consequences. In most human communities, assertions of identity are encouraged while more nuanced, more balanced, more ecumenical attitudes are deemed naive, timorous, or even suspect. Many of those who were long at the forefront of the struggle for universality have found themselves disoriented. One only has to look at the countries that were once the beacons of all mankind to assess the extent of the damage.

I am thinking in particular of the Netherlands and the Scandinavian countries, countries which pioneered openness and tolerance, and have found such a stance increasingly difficult to maintain. I am thinking of Great Britain, whose political system, long a model for the rest of the world, is being shattered by a nationalist populism that borders on fraud. And I am also thinking of Italy, whose politics and culture were revered and admired by my generation, and which is now all but unrecognizable.

Are we simply dealing with a series of visceral, knee-jerk reactions triggered by tensions that will abate over time? Or is this a long-term phenomenon, one that may prove difficult to reverse, and lead all mankind into a spiral of violence?

Personally, I feel that, over recent decades, we have shifted from a fleeting reaction to a long-term mindset. We have switched from a scenario, all too common in the past, where communities living cheek by jowl begin to mistrust each other and come to blows, only for tensions to subside and the communities to forget they were ever enemies, to a scenario where this kind of "happy ending" is no longer on the agenda.

There have been a number of determining factors for this sea change: beginning with the political and moral upheavals that have rocked the Arab world since its defeat in 1967; which were then further aggravated by the conservative revolutions in both East and West that began around 1979; until finally, the events of September 11, 2001, sent the whole world into a "tailspin," setting off the chain reaction that is now leading us into the unknown—and most likely towards disaster.

One of the most disturbing aspects of this sea change has been the "Orwellian drift" that the world now faces. My apologies to Orwell, but I feel that it is a tribute to name a disease after the scientist who first identified it— one who did everything in his power to fight it.

7

George Orwell was a bitter enemy of totalitarianism, and tried to alert his contemporaries to the tyrannies ahead, to the ways in which modern tools would be used to crush all human freedom and dignity. His harrowing moral tale, 1984, was bound to grab people's attention and force them to think. Were we drifting towards a world in which Big Brother could hear and see everything, even our innermost thoughts? A world where language would be so controlled, so distorted, that it would be impossible to express opinions that did not conform to official ideology? A world in which every gesture, every thought, every feeling could be monitored and judged by an omnipotent authority that claimed to act in the best interests of humankind?

Born in 1903, Orwell witnessed the rise of the two major totalitarian regimes of the century, led by Stalin and Hitler. He fought both of them; by physically taking up arms alongside the Spanish Republicans, and through his writings. He was alive to celebrate the defeat of Nazism, but when he died—prematurely, of tuberculosis, in 1950—the other totalitarian regime was still expanding. Stalin still clung firmly to the reins of power, buoyed up by the prestige of his victory in the Second World War; his forces occupied half of Europe; the Soviet Union had just succeeded in making an atomic bomb; and the outcome of the Cold War was far from certain. The nightmare described by Orwell in 1984 was based on the idea of a Stalinist regime dominating the whole world, and in particular, Britain.

If he had had better medical treatment, Orwell might have survived to see the year he gave as a title to his novel and beyond, to see the collapse of the Soviet Union. We might have celebrated with him, rather than paying him posthumous tribute. And he would have had every reason to celebrate, since the threat he warned people against looked as though it had been permanently defeated.

These days, things look much less certain. Big Brother walked out the door only to creep back in through the window. His return is not the result of some new totalitarian power, but of a phenomenon that is more diffuse, and more pernicious: the inexorable rise of our obsession with security.

With what little hindsight I can muster as I write, it already seems clear that the world post-9/11 will never again be as it was before. The war on terrorism is different from all those that came before it, including both World Wars and the Cold War, in that it has no designated end. It is as though we had declared war on sin or on evil. There will be no post-war period. There will never again come a time when we can let our guard down and say that the danger has passed. Especially if we look at what is happening in the Arab-Muslim world. When will it find peace and stability? All we can say for certain is that it will be many decades before the situation has any chance of being resolved.

What lies ahead is a long period of turmoil, punctuated by attacks, massacres, and atrocities, one that will be dangerous and traumatic; a period during which, despite the protestations of the current administration, a power such as that of the United States will be forced to protect itself, hunt down its enemies, intercept their telephone conversations, monitor their internet activity, check their financial transactions ...

This is inevitable, and government overreach cannot be avoided. While the stated aim of such surveillance is to prevent the funding of terrorist groups, it also offers an opportunity to check whether US citizens are evading taxes. What is the connection between terrorism and tax evasion? There is none. Except that, once a government has the necessary technology and the perfect excuse to monitor people, it will monitor people.

The government's stated aim is to intercept terrorist communications, but they will take the opportunity to eavesdrop on commercial rivals. What is the connection between the phone calls made by a bomber and those made by a French, Korean, or Italian industrialist? There is none. Except that, if the government has an excuse to wiretap communications that might benefit American companies, it will wiretap those communications. It will even eavesdrop on the private conversations of German, Brazilian, Indian, or Japanese leaders; and if they should find out, it will apologize and go back to monitoring their calls while taking a few extra precautions so that no one finds out.

I have talked about the United States, but this is true, or will shortly be true, of Russia, China, India, France, and any other country capable of acquiring the necessary tools.

It is almost a law of human nature: whatever science makes it possible for us to do, we will do, sooner or later, on some pretext or other. At least for as long as the benefits appear to outweigh the risks.

*

Having voiced these concerns, and before I move on to others, I would like to point out that, happily, the world we live in today is not like the one described in Orwell's novel.

For the moment, any fears we might harbour have to do with the potential dangers. The constant monitoring to which our contemporaries are subjected may elicit frustration, amazement, and sometimes even justifiable outrage; but it does not inspire terror like the collapse of the Twin Towers in Manhattan, the kidnapping of Nigerian schoolgirls by the sinister Boko Haram, or the public beheadings of Daesh. Faced with such atrocities, our other fears inevitably pale into insignificance.

However, we would be mistaken to underestimate the inherent risks of Orwellian drift, because it has certain characteristics that ultimately make it highly pernicious.

While the acts of murderous savagery we are witnessing can make us believe that we are reverting to the dark days of the past, in actual fact the drift that Orwell warned about comes from the future. This drift is made possible by scientific advances and technological innovations, which governments turn to their own nefarious uses. We believe we are moving forward, when in fact we are adrift. Progress is being made in many areas, these days people live better and longer lives. But something has been lost along the way. The freedom to come and go as we please, to speak and to write without being constantly monitored.

Like petrol from a leaking tank, our freedom is trickling away, drop by drop, without our even noticing. Everything seems normal. We can carry on driving, humming as we go. Until the engine eventually gives out. And the car comes to a grinding halt.

I have cited the monitoring of telephone calls and bank transactions as something that even the most democratic governments may be tempted to do. But these are simply examples of a drift that goes much further, one that we can see occurring in our everyday lives.

I sometimes exchange emails with friends who are writers or composers. And in recent years, I have noticed a regular phenomenon: while I am writing to them, or reading an email from them, a pop-up appears on my screen suggesting I buy their books or their CDs. The same thing happens if, in my email, I mention Simone de Beauvoir, Saul Bellow, or Robert Musil. Instantly I get a pop-up offering to sell me their books.

The first time I noticed this, I was puzzled, even angry; since then, I have grown accustomed to it—though that does not mean I approve of the process. In order to function, such a process would need swift, immediate access to what I am typing, and the ability to analyse keywords and instantly display onscreen a message generated by my private correspondence.

I will not go into technical details; I do not know enough about the technology and, besides, things are changing so quickly that what seems innovative today will probably be obsolete two years from now. That will not change the fact that, increasingly, every sentence we type on a computer, every word we speak into the phone, every digital picture we take and store, will be accessible to strangers who have the means to analyse, store, and use them at will.

In addition to being monitored, at every moment of the day, we can be tracked and even filmed thanks to our mobile phones, CCTV cameras, drones, satellites, and a host of other sophisticated gadgets that will surely be invented. As a result it is possible to know precisely who met whom, what they said, where they spent the night, and countless other details.

Personally, none of this particularly bothers me on a day-to-day basis. I know that the software analysing the content of my emails and generating pop-ups are simply algorithms, that it is unlikely an actual human being is attempting to spy on me. I am not secretive by nature, so I do not much care if someone knows where I buy my books, my wine, or my shirts, or where I spend my nights.

But there is no need to weave a dystopian fantasy to realize that the tools allowing authorities to intrude on our private lives today could lead to outrageous abuses in the future. Whether we are talking about government agencies attempting to monitor the political opinions of its citizens, or private companies attempting to amass the endless details we provide about ourselves—what we call "big data"—so they can sell on this information at exorbitant prices. Everything becomes a commodity: our tastes, our opinions, our habits, our health, our contact details and those of our friends and acquaintances, all the minutiae of our lives.

We could endlessly debate the extent to which this "data capture" is actually harmful, rather than being simply an irritating but harmless feature of the modern world. Personally, I believe it is harmful, and likely to lead us down a slippery slope.

*

Every day the line between what is private and what is public in our lives fades a little more. All too often we are complicit in this contraction of our private sphere. In our desire to communicate, to please, to be like other people, out of either resignation or ignorance, we allow ourselves to be invaded. We rarely try to differentiate between those things that enrich us and those that leave us poorer, those that free and those that enslave.

We possess increasingly sophisticated technologies that make us feel like we are wealthy and powerful; but they are akin to the electronic tags worn by prisoners on probation. Or like a leash we wear around our necks, oblivious to who is holding the other end.

It is hardly surprising that, for some, this drift is reminiscent of the obsessive universe of 1984, where countless eyes track people through the streets, in their offices, into their homes on behalf of Big Brother and the Thought Police.

8

Since my teenage years, I have been fascinated by the works of Orwell, while casting a critical and selective eye over them. I have always considered that his great masterpiece is *Animal Farm*; I was always less engaged by *1984*. The idea behind *1984* was undeniably powerful; but, as so often with novels that expound a social or political thesis, the novel is somewhat overshadowed by the thesis. Moreover, when I first began to pay attention to world events, Stalin was dead, his body had been removed from the mausoleum in Red Square, and Stalingrad had been renamed; the threat of Stalinism that the novel warned against no longer seemed plausible, and its message of alarm appeared unwarranted.

I made my peace with *1984* the day I realized that the most important thing in a literary work is not the message the author is trying to convey, but the intellectual and emotional sustenance each reader can draw from it. When I reread the novel as an adult, I became keenly aware that all human societies, however developed, ran the risk of being caught up in a system that would challenge everything that they had built.

Granted, the form that this threat takes today is not the one that Orwell feared. His imagination was conditioned by the era in which he lived; having observed the totalitarian regimes of his age, he believed he knew where future tyrannies would come from, the ideologies that would govern them, and the methods they would use to survive. If, in this, he was mistaken, in the main he was nonetheless correct. Because, beyond his hatred of dictatorships, whether left- or right-wing, he had a more fundamental fear, that of seeing science perverted, ideals warped, and human beings enslaved by the very things that were supposed to free them.

It is this dread that comes through in his writings. A dread that is as justified today as it was then, sadly. Not because of the totalitarian nightmare that obsessed him, but because of a different nightmare, one that would doubtless have horrified him had he imagined it.

A frightened world in which constant surveillance of our every action is dictated by a real and legitimate need to feel protected at every moment is ultimately more disturbing than a world where surveillance is imposed by a paranoid and authoritarian regime.

In Orwell's mind, the name "Big Brother" was bitterly ironic, like the nickname sometimes given to Stalin, "The Father of Nations." To characterise the relationship between oppressor and victim as "brotherly" or "fatherly" requires a twisted worldview. Yet those of us living in the twenty-first century do not think of the electronic eyes that follow us everywhere as hostile.

Faced with the twisted world around us, we increasingly feel the need to know that we are safe. As a result, we do not see those responsible for this surveillance as oppressors, but as genuine "big brothers." By and large, the electronic eyes following us have no sinister purpose; their intrusions into our private world usually result from a drift that is trailing technologies and people in its wake.

I have already said that such intrusions into my day-to-day life do not bother me particularly. On the whole, I have adapted to them, and can even sometimes see the benefits. I assume this is the same for most of my contemporaries. We are relieved when we hear that a criminal has been captured using CCTV footage, or that a corrupt leader has been brought down using information from his itemized phone bills.

It is only when we become aware of some outrageous invasion of our own privacy that we begin to balk and become indignant. But our indignation is short-lived, and measured. As though our ability to react has been numbed.

Were it not for the circumstances in which we live these days, these infringements on our freedom would provoke outrage. The idea that someone was listening to our calls, filming our comings and goings, would seem totally unacceptable; that in airports we are scanned and frisked and forced to remove our shoes and our belts would seem blatantly insulting; citizens' rights groups would be campaigning to impose strict limits on such intrusions.

But this is not how we have reacted. Daring an analogy with biology, I would say that the world events of recent decades have had the effect of "blocking" us from "secreting antibodies." We are less shocked than we should be by these infringements on our freedoms; we protest, though only feebly. We place our trust in the authorities protecting us; and if they go too far, we claim extenuating circumstances.

This dulling of our critical faculties is, in my view, a significant and very worrying development.

I have made reference to the system into which this century we have been dragged. Using the analogy of "antibodies," we can more closely observe how the system works: the rise of identity-related tensions triggers legitimate fears, this causes us to seek security for ourselves and our loved ones at all costs, and to be vigilant whenever we feel threatened. As a result, we are less aware of the potential abuses that this heightened state of vigilance can lead to; less wary when technology infringes on our privacy; less vigilant when governments amend laws in ways that are increasingly peremptory and authoritarian; less alert to the risks of Orwellian drift ...

*

In every generation, it is necessary to strike a balance between protecting people from those who exploit democracy in order to erode personal freedoms, and also from those who, on the pretext of protecting democracy, seek to weaken it. At the present time, I feel that it is a balance we have succeeded in maintaining. The future, however, looks much less reassuring. We are caught in a process that is infantilizing and potentially enslaving, one that will prove difficult to curb; new technological advances will only serve the ability of governments to intrude on their citizens, while the fears used to justify such intrusions are unlikely to disappear. Some see this as an insidious process, one that, if not totalitarian, is at best manipulative and authoritarian; personally, I see it as the sad but inevitable result of the demons of identity politics we have unleashed on the world and are now unable to tame.

This calamitous dynamic could get worse and go beyond that which we can imagine today. I cannot bring myself to imagine how our contemporaries would react if our cities were to suffer massive attacks involving biological, chemical, or nuclear weapons.

I hope we can avoid such catastrophes, but sadly it is not unreasonable to think that they might occur, and, if so, their impact on our societies would be devastating.

Even if it were possible to indefinitely delay such atrocities, the drift would continue. In recent opinion polls, whether in Europe, the United States, or elsewhere, we have seen that voters are more likely to listen to those voices who insist that we have to protect ourselves by any means necessary, than to those who warn against our obsession with security and our excessive use of force. The results of these polls are understandable in a world where people fear that they may be a target, where they feel vulnerable; what remains to be seen is how far we can go in our need to feel safe without undermining other, equally legitimate, freedoms.

We have only to look around us to realize that the way of the world is unlikely to allay these fears.

In all honesty, I cannot think of a single scenario in which this trend might be reversed. Every indication suggests that it will continue, sometimes more slowly, sometimes more quickly, but always tending in the same direction: a steady increase of fear.

What will our countries look like in twenty years, in fifty years? I wish I could say that I believe these shifts in our political and intellectual landscape will prove ephemeral, that our concerns over terrorism or migration will be temporary, that our societies will come through these ordeals more generous, more tolerant, more magnanimous. But that is not what is looming on the horizon. There is a very real fear that our contemporaries and their descendants will increasingly listen to those voices that say it is better to live in a heavily guarded fortress with high walls, even if that means sacrificing certain freedoms and values.

"The choice for mankind lies between freedom and happiness, and for the great bulk of mankind, happiness is better," Orwell has one of his characters say cynically in 1984. No one else is likely to present the situation to us quite as bluntly; but in the century in which we find ourselves, this dilemma no longer sounds completely outrageous.

9

If I have discussed the "Orwellian" drift at length, it is because it poses a threat to the future of democracy, to the rule of law as the set of values that give meaning to human experience. But this threat, terrifying as it is, is not the only one that now looms on the horizon. In a crumbling world where the sacrosanct egotism of tribes, individuals, and clans now prevails, situations become increasingly complex and fester until they become intractable.

One example among many—and one of the most significant—is that of climate change. In recent decades, scientists have been warning us about global warming and its potentially catastrophic effects: vast swathes of land either flooded or plagued by drought, resulting in the mass migration of people; a rise in temperatures that might prove impossible to curb, making the Earth uninhabitable.

We are consistently warned that the measures taken so far to prevent the disaster are insufficient, that their impact is negligible, that warning signs are coming thick and fast: glaciers are melting more quickly than anticipated, ocean currents are behaving erratically, extreme weather events are occurring at an unprecedented rate. And, as each year ends, we are told that it was amongst the hottest on record.

I realize that there are still climate sceptics, and I am not arguing that debate should not continue, but faced with the mounting concern of so many respected scientists and academics, we must at least consider the idea that they might not be wrong.

To be perfectly honest, I hope that they are wrong. Because if, as I fear, their hypotheses are correct, then—given the current state of world events—catastrophe seems inevitable. Some world leaders dismiss scientists' warnings as the bleating of people motivated by anti-globalist views, and insist we should focus on economic performance; others believe that *their* country has already done enough, and that those more industrialized countries or those with higher rates of pollution must shoulder their share of the burden; still others are content to trot out worthy statements, or measures that will play well in the media, with little concern for their actual effects ...

Whatever the reasons invoked for doing nothing, or for doing as little as possible, it seems clear that in the world in which we live, characterized as it is by the increasing distrust of international organizations and the glorification of the ethos of every man for himself, is utterly incapable of marshalling the solidarity necessary to deal with a threat of this magnitude.

One day, we will look back in horror at the fact that, on a Saturday evening in December 2018, as riots raged on the streets of Paris, the President of the United States publicly celebrated the fact that the riots had occurred in the city where the International Climate Change Agreement was signed.

To the threat posed by climate change we should add another, one that, while not unfamiliar to students of history, is equally worrying: the arms race. Despite having abated after the collapse of the Soviet Union, a new arms race has begun, pitting those countries that dream of becoming global powers against the United States, which is determined to prevent them.

China, a vast nation that has grown exponentially in recent decades, naturally has ambitions to play a leading role on the world stage. It has the necessary manpower, financial resources, and industrial capacity, and is rapidly catching up in terms of military technology. It also has a political system capable of long-term planning, a rare thing in the world these days.

The rivalry between Beijing and Washington, whose initial tensions we can already see, will be harsh; it will take the form of trade wars, of confrontation in media conflicts, in diplomacy, in cybernetics, and it is already marked by an all-out arms race both on land and in space.

Russia also intends to reassert itself, and to reclaim its dominant role on the world stage. Having emerged from the Cold War bankrupt, humiliated, and demoralized, it is now attempting to regain lost ground—politically, as it has in Syria, and geographically, as it has in the Crimea. Moscow is engaged in a trial of strength on several fronts, not merely with Washington, but with the West in general.

Aside from these historic superpowers, there are other countries vying to play a more dominant role—whether regional or global—and they too are engaged in the arms race. I am thinking particularly of India, Pakistan, Turkey, Iran, and Israel, to say nothing of France and Germany, South Korea and Japan.

Such a "free-for-all" is not unprecedented. In every century, we have witnessed countries battling to assert their power while others counterattack, reconquer, or are forced to retreat and collapse, and in earlier times such battles were more bloody and brutal than they are today.

What makes our era more dangerous is that, as technology has advanced, potentially lethal knowledge has spread across the globe, resulting in new weapons of mass destruction being devised. Many countries already possess or are trying to acquire such weapons, so too are extremist movements and even organized crime syndicates.

As a consequence, mistakes and blunders will be harder to avoid, and their consequences are potentially devastating. How can one not be terrified at the thought of "dirty bombs" capable of dispersing radioactive substances that could contaminate vast areas for decades; or worse, the phials of biological weapons whose contents, we are told, could wipe out the population of a city?

So many players around the world dream of ridding themselves of their sworn enemies once and for all, and it is possible to imagine the circumstances in which they might act. All we can do is hope that they never have the opportunity.

*

What humanity does best is warped by what it does worst—this is the tragic paradox of our time, and it is true in many areas.

In a disintegrating world, even the most promising medical advances, those most beneficial to the future of the species, can become dangerous. If, tomorrow, science succeeded in manipulating the process of cell ageing and organ replacement, thereby extending life expectancy, it would be a truly amazing development. But it would also be terrifying, since, for at least two or three generations, such expensive techniques would benefit only a tiny fraction of the global population. And this minority, the "chosen," would break away to form a different humanity, with much longer lifespans than their ordinary contemporaries. How would the world cope with such a disparity, one that would represent the culmination of inequality? Would those who could not afford to extend their lifespan simply accept their fate? Or would it rather fuel their anger and their thirst for revenge?

And what of the privileged few? Would they not be tempted to barricade themselves behind high walls and ruthlessly eliminate anyone who threatened them?

This may seem like a remote prospect, but there is a similar threat, one that is more immediate and is even now being developed. I am referring to the extraordinary advances in artificial intelligence, in terms of robotics and miniaturization, resulting in complex tasks, once undertaken by people, being transferred to increasingly sophisticated machines.

The roots of this date back to the beginnings of the industrial revolution, at which time mechanization, though widely criticized and even demonized, nevertheless proved beneficial, since it had reduced costs and was able to boost production while freeing up the workforce from the most menial tasks. But what is happening now is of a different order. It is no longer simply routine tasks that are being replicated, but the extraordinary complexity of human intelligence that is being reproduced and gradually surpassed.

As we all know, the greatest chess player in the world today is a computer, as is the greatest player of Go. And these are just two small flags planted on the tip of the iceberg.

The steady replacement of man by machine is something that can be observed daily in all spheres of activity, whether transport, trade, agriculture, medicine, or, demonstrably, industrial production. There are already robot drivers, robot delivery services, robot receptionists, bank tellers, surgeons, customs officers, etc. The list is endless, and, as research progresses, it will continue to grow. Everything suggests that in the future "our robot cousins" will be ubiquitous in our homes, our streets, in offices, shops, and factories.

I am using the term "robot," even though it is not always appropriate. Machines that possess a certain degree of intelligence or skill do not necessarily take on a human form, and while some have arms and legs, a head, and even a voice, many others are simply flickering clanking machines. But the word "robot," which has since been adopted by many languages, still retains the mythic sense it had when Karel Čapek first coined the term in his play *Rossum's Universal Robots*: a humanoid creature created by mankind in order to carry out tasks that we find arduous, unpleasant, or physically impossible.

In the future, if we decide to explore Mars, Jupiter, Saturn, or more distant planets far beyond our solar system, what astronauts could we send if not robots? Robots could accomplish missions lasting thirty or even eighty years in atmospheric conditions that would be unendurable for human beings. Only robots could establish a permanent base on our moon without having to worry about the lack of oxygen.

The epic of human space flight would be reduced to a memory of a brief heroic moment, the first faltering expeditions.

It is likely that something similar will occur in the military sector, at least in those countries that have the resources. Why send their soldiers to their deaths when the same tasks could be performed by robots and drones? It may seem as though I am straying into science fiction, but this is an issue that a number of countries are already studying. One on which researchers are already working.

Granted, there are certain tasks a human soldier can perform better than a robot. But the reverse is also true. A robot can be programmed to move at a hundred kilometres an hour, it can be the size of a squirrel, or an elephant, or a rat. Most importantly, it has the advantage that if it "dies" in battle, it will not trouble anyone on the home front. There would be no body bags, no coffins draped with the national flag, no grieving families, no traumatized veterans, no demonstrations demanding that we repatriate "our children." Of course, there would still be fatalities in the enemy camp, but that is a different problem, and one that leaders would have no trouble dealing with through politics and the media.

We often reassure ourselves by thinking that behind every robot, however sophisticated, there is still a human hand, a human brain. Perhaps; but that is not the issue. It is not a matter of whether the Human, capital *H*, will continue to be necessary; it is about *how many* humans we will need in twenty, or forty years. If the current trend in robotics continues, hundreds of millions of jobs will disappear, and within a few short decades, only a small fraction of our fellow humans will still be involved in the production of wealth.

What would become of the others, of the billions of others? Excluded from the workplace, marginalized, and literally "abandoned," how would they survive? Would the "useful" minority support them in the name of human solidarity? Or would that minority consider them superfluous, a burden, parasitic, and potentially dangerous?

The very notion of humanity, patiently built up over thousands of years, would become meaningless.

*

I have listed only the dangers that may face us during this century. I could list so many others ...

Some were bound to arise one day, since they are a direct result of scientific progress; others are due to the aberrations we have experienced in recent decades.

What is clear is that we have entered an era that is turbulent, unpredictable, hazardous, and that is destined to continue for a long time. The majority of our contemporaries no longer believe in a future based on progress and prosperity. Wherever they find themselves, they are helpless, angry, bitter, disoriented. And, mistrustful of the whirling world around them, they are tempted to trust in dangerous fantasists.

Caught in this maelstrom, everything is now possible, and no country, no institution, no value system, no civilization seems capable of navigating the turbulence and emerging unscathed.

Epilogue

No siempre lo peor es cierto.
(The worst is not always certain.)

Pedro Calderón de la Barca (1600–1681)

When I began this meditation on the unsettling times in which I have lived, I resolved to speak personally only when I had been a witness to events—either directly or via those closest to me—and only if I felt a first-person narrative might shed some light on the subject. I was determined not to stray from my role as an observer, or to attach undue importance to my personal view.

More than once, I even paused between chapters to make sure I was not the victim of an "optical illusion," that it truly was the world that was adrift, and not simply *my* world—the lost Egypt of my mother, my father's Lebanon, the Arab civilization of my youth, the world of my adoptive country, of Europe, and my heroic universalist ideals. But every time I returned to my writing persuaded that, sadly, I was not mistaken.

No, what I am expressing is not nostalgia, but my concern for the future, my justifiable fear of seeing my children, my grandchildren, and their contemporaries living in a nightmarish world. And also, my fear of witnessing the disappearance of everything that gives meaning to the human adventure.

In the very first sentence of this book, when I spoke of being born into a dying civilization, I was not thinking simply of the Levant, though it is perhaps a little closer to death than other civilizations; it was always a fragile, shimmering, evanescent culture, and now it lies in ruins. But it is not the only culture to which I belong, the only one that nurtured me, or the only one that is foundering today.

Regarding the civilization I was born into, I feel it important to add that if its demise has been a tragedy for those of us who grew up there, it is scarcely less so for the rest of the world. I firmly believe that if the pluralistic Levant could have survived, thrived, and flourished, all of humanity, every civilization, could have avoided the drift that we are witnessing today.

It is from my native land that the shadows spread and engulfed the world.

I would have been hesitant to write that last sentence a few years ago, I would have felt that I was crudely extrapolating from my personal experience and that of my family. Now, there can be no doubt that the convulsions which have shaken the planet are directly related to those that have shaken the Arab world in recent decades.

I would not go so far as to say that the flames which engulfed downtown Cairo in January 1952 and those that, half a century later, engulfed the Twin Towers in New York are part of the same fire. But it obvious to everyone now that there is a connection, a cause and effect, between the collapse of "my" native Levant and that of other civilizations.

In my seventy years on earth, I have witnessed, directly or indirectly, an endless series of events. I survey them now as though they were all part of a single fresco. I see the lines of force, the confusion of colours, the grey areas, the convolutions, and I feel better able to "decode" the universe that surrounds me.

I will not deny that I have rashly assigned precise dates to complex changes; as, for example, when I wrote that the despair of the Arab world began on June 5, 1967, or that 1979 was "the year of the great reversal" in the world. I could have limited myself to phrases that were more vague and less open to attack. But I favoured urgency, effectiveness, and clarity. I trusted my intuition as a close and attentive witness, hoping that the grains of truth in my rash assertions might prove useful for those who truly want to understand the tragedy now looming on the horizon.

*

In conjuring the spectre of drift, of imminent shipwreck, am I not running the risk of encouraging readers to give up hope?

It is certainly not my intention to foster despair, but I feel that in the grave circumstances we are faced with in this century, it is the duty of everyone to be lucid, sincere, and truthful. Anyone who denies the gravity of the dangers that face us, or underestimates the ruthlessness of the world in order to assuage the fears of others, runs the risk of being quickly refuted by events.

If the roads that lie ahead are treacherous, the worst thing we can do is to drive on with our eyes closed, muttering that everything will be fine.

What is more, I am convinced that change is possible. I cannot bring myself to believe that humanity will meekly resign itself to the destruction of everything it has created. If this drift continues, all human societies and civilizations stand to lose, just as all stand to gain if we can change course. When we finally accept this fact, our behaviour will radically change, the drift will be curbed, and a more favourable course will begin.

As a result, it is necessary, indeed crucial, to alert, to explain, to exhort, and to warn; without lapsing into apathy, complacency, or disillusionment. And, most importantly, without resorting to aggression. Constantly bearing in mind that the tragedies happening today are the result of a chain of events that no one can control, one that is dragging us in its wake, the rich and the poor, the weak and the powerful, the citizens and those who govern them, oblivious to our wishes, regardless of our affiliations, our origins, or our opinions.

Beyond the urgent clamour of current events, beyond the deafening roar of this century, there is a single preoccupation that should guide our thoughts and actions: how do we persuade our contemporaries that by remaining prisoner to the tribal concepts of identity, nation, or religion, by continuing to glorify egotism and individualism, they are creating an apocalyptic future for their children?

In a world in which so many different peoples live cheek by jowl, in which so many lethal weapons are in countless hands, we cannot allow individual passion and greed to have free rein. To imagine that some "collective survival instinct" will magically defuse these dangers is not evidence of optimism or faith in the future, but of denial, blindness, and irresponsibility.

*

In recent years, we have had telling glimpses and sometimes painful illustrations of each of the dangers mentioned in this book—like a foretaste of what could happen if the drift goes unchecked. Will we learn our lessons before these catastrophes hit us hard? Will we have the moral strength to pull ourselves together and to right the ship before it is too late?

I still want to hope so. It would be heartrending if the ship of mankind continued to sail towards disaster, oblivious to danger, convinced it is unsinkable, much like the *Titanic*—only to plough into the iceberg and sink into the darkness while the band played "Nearer, My God, to Thee," and the champagne continued to flow.

Postface

I write these last pages during the unsettling spring of 2020, a year after this essay was first published in France, at a time when the world is faced with one of the most devastating challenges in human history.

How will this nightmare end? Who among us will be victims and who will come through it unscathed? Which countries and institutions, which dogmas and values, will come through weakened and which will emerge stronger than before? Only in hindsight will we be able to measure the full consequences of what we are currently going through. Nevertheless, we can say without fear of contradiction that the events of this year will not be soon forgotten; that, for many years to come we will speak of a "pre-" and a "post-"2020; and that the future of the planet will be profoundly and permanently affected.

One of the major characteristics of the COVID-19 pandemic is that, over and above the medical and scientific considerations, it constitutes a serious challenge to the way in which every country is governed, and the relationships between the various groups that make up humanity.

In itself, the virus does not seem to be as deadly as some we have seen in recent years, such as Ebola and HIV. Even in these first weeks, it has proved possible to treat the great majority of those infected, and we can reasonably assume that effective remedies, together with a vaccine, will be rapidly developed. The major worry is that coronavirus is highly contagious and many of those affected suffer respiratory symptoms that require intensive care. If the rate of infection cannot be slowed, then without the correct equipment, or without sufficient equipment, people are quickly faced with cruel and impossible decisions: if there are twelve ventilators and thirty patients currently in critical condition, who should be kept alive and who should be allowed to die? To this, one must add a further dilemma, one that is less poignant but no less serious: while the virus is spreading rapidly, should governments force their citizens to abide by guidelines, or leave them some measure of freedom?

Such issues go far beyond the sphere of medicine. They force us to ask a broader question, one that will haunt our thoughts, our conversations, and our debates for years to come: how should human societies function in order to be able to face such challenges? In a sense, the current pandemic is a "stress test" for every country on earth. If we are to encounter other deadly threats in the future—whether caused by armed conflict, terrorist attacks, nuclear accidents, or climate catastrophes— how should we best organize ourselves in order to face them? What changes should we make to our behaviours, to our habits, to our relationships with our fellow creatures, whether near or far?

The world that will emerge from the current crisis exists only in embryo, and it would be presumptuous to try to say what it will look like. But certain facets are already apparent.

It seems likely, for example, that the habits acquired during months of confinement and social distancing will not disappear completely when this is over. Either because we will have discovered unforeseen advantages to them, or because the fear that the pandemic will return, in our own country or in others around the world, will urge a more permanent prudence. New norms may be established that, for many among us, will change the way we work or eat, the way we care for others or entertain ourselves; our way of meeting others and greeting them; our ways of travelling or not travelling. We may witness the emergence of a world in which digitization and automation accelerate unimpeded, where people increasingly meet in videoconferences, where we spend less time in public places, train stations, and airports, where we favour products that can be obtained without the need for contact with other human beings.

The consequences of such an evolution could be simultaneously calamitous and beneficial. A substantial decrease in mass consumption could indefinitely prolong the economic crisis that will follow the pandemic, leaving millions unemployed. But it could also reduce atmospheric pollution, reduce the waste of natural resources, and improve the prospects for the future of the planet.

There may also be significant changes to the way in which human societies are governed.

In the preceding essay, I talked at length about the conservative revolution triggered by Margaret Thatcher in 1979, which played a crucial role in the "great reversal" the world has since experienced. One of the major aspects of this revolution was its questioning of the role of government. We should not expect government to solve our problems, we were told, because government was the problem, as in the oft-quoted maxim of Ronald Reagan. The ideology that has prevailed for the past four decades, initially in the United Kingdom and the United States and later in numerous countries around the world, was that it was essential to significantly reduce the state's role in economic affairs and its role in social policy. There would be no more "welfare state" taking care of disadvantaged minorities, ensuring they had food and housing and health care. There were even attempts to limit the government's role in law and order, with the management of prisons transferred to private companies.

The limitations of this vision of the world became apparent during what we might come to call the "great fear of 2020." For several weeks, a number of world leaders were tempted not to stem the spread of the pandemic, but to allow it to move through the population so that it would acquire "herd immunity," which would protect it from further outbreaks of the virus. This theory, which had its defenders within the scientific community, is somewhat reminiscent of Adam Smith's "invisible hand," and it is easy to understand why the heirs to Thatcher and Reagan would have considered adopting it. Would it not be better to allow nature, in its wisdom, to resolve the problem, they reasoned, rather than attempting to thwart its plans? Would it not be better to carry on working, producing, living as before, taking a few simple precautions, while waiting for the epidemic to burn itself out, as happens every year with seasonal flu? In doing so, might it not be possible to avert an economic collapse whose human toll might be even greater than that of the pandemic?

Such questions—clearly expressed in Washington, in London, in Stockholm, and in Amsterdam—explain the prevarications of Donald Trump, who, at the outset, sought to minimise the health risks. But this laissez-faire policy proved politically untenable, as he himself admitted in a press conference at the White House on March 31: when warned by experts that allowing the virus free rein could lead to more than two million deaths in the United States in the space of a few weeks, he was forced to abandon his risky strategy and advocate confinement.

Does this mean that the crisis has sounded the death knell for the conservative revolution that has flourished for the past forty years? It is too early to say with any degree of certainty, but it is true that the pandemic has profoundly undermined the credibility of the worldview promoted by advocates of economic liberalism.

This worldview had been increasingly challenged in recent years. Protests and demonstrations have erupted in countries around the world—from Chile to Indonesia by way of France—denouncing the failings of a system that has exacerbated inequality, impoverished the middle classes, and vastly increased the number of "those left behind." While it has unquestionably favoured a period of global economic expansion, there have been signs that governments based on the primacy of market forces were running out of steam. People realized that corrections were needed to temper its excesses and make it more humane. The tragedy of 2020 has demonstrated that, if applied too strictly, too blindly, the consequences of Thatcherism could be monstrous. Particularly in the domain of healthcare. Years of savage budget cuts in a sector that, while not productive, is literally *vital*, led to substantial shortages of staff and medical equipment, and this has resulted in a cataclysm that has gravely compromised the moral legitimacy of economic liberalism.

It is reasonable to suppose that, on the contrary, the role of government in protecting those it governs has reclaimed a legitimacy it seemed to have lost. After such a health crisis, it will not be as easy to mock the "nanny state" as it was before. Especially since governments will inevitably have to play a major role in kick-starting an economy crippled by the pandemic. After the current crash, just as after the crash of 1929, there will have to be a large-scale "new deal," which only governments will have the means to fund and manage.

But it is not only the proponents of economic liberalism who have seen their credibility weakened by the "great fear of 2020." The West as a whole is emerging from the ordeal battered, bruised, and discredited. Because it has shown neither moral leadership nor technical efficiency. At a moment when the whole of humanity was threatened and looking to be reassured, comforted, supported, guided, neither the United States nor Europe rose to the challenge. They seemed overwhelmed, at a loss, and occasionally pitiful.

Will the West, which for centuries has played the principal role on the world stage, be replaced by other actors from the South or from the East, as has been suggested since the beginning of this crisis? I do not believe so. What we are witnessing is the dissolution of any world order worthy of the name. The most plausible scenario is not one power being replaced by another, like a new sovereign might claim the throne vacated by a predecessor. On the contrary, we should expect a long and tumultuous "interregnum," punctuated by conflicts of all kinds, before a new equilibrium can be established.

*

One of the most regrettable spectacles we have been forced to witness since the onset of the pandemic is the torrent of abuse and accusations that Europe and the United States have launched across the Atlantic, and within their own countries. With allies and partners calling each other "modern pirates" and "shameless prof-iteers," "gangsters" and "thieves." In reading the news, we learn that a cargo destined for patients in one European country was seized and rerouted in favour of another. That an urgent request for masks and ventilators from one state was met with a refusal from its nearest neigh-bours. And that an American manufacturer was pre-vented from fulfilling a duly signed contract to provide medical equipment to a European country; and when it challenged the prohibition, it was dubbed unpatriotic and practically accused of high treason for not according its fellow citizens absolute priority. How far we have come from the Europe envisaged by its founders and the America of the Marshall Plan.

It is true that, historically, pandemics have always pushed people towards isolation rather than openness. People shut themselves away, they close their borders, surround themselves with barriers—both literal and figurative. They become suspicious of anyone who comes from elsewhere—a different country, a different prov-ince, even a different village. It is a perfectly understand-able reaction when people feel they are in mortal danger.

What remains to be seen is whether normal behaviour will resume once the crisis has passed and the great fear has abated. I hope with all my heart that it will, but I am far from certain. Because these new suspicions have fallen on fertile ground. In Europe, the self-interest we have witnessed since the beginning of the crisis has come at a moment when the dream of unity is already fractured and badly in need of a demonstration of fraternity if it is to be repaired. The way in which the pandemic has so far been handled will do little to allay the mistrust among the peoples of Europe.

And the same can be said on a global scale. The already tense relationships between America, China, Russia, Europe, or Iran have led to acrimonious exchanges over who should bear the blame for what has happened. Poisonous rumours flourish on social networks ... Here, too, mistrust will not soon fade. In a world where entrenched and aggressive identity politics has prevailed for decades, the great fear of 2020 and the economic crisis that will follow it are unlikely to bring people closer together or to foster mutual consideration and solidarity.

The argument I have just put forward is one that I would also make for the emergency measures that have been taken to deal with the pandemic, and which have routinely trampled on public freedoms and on private lives.

In ordinary circumstances, such extreme measures would be temporary and, when the crisis ends—just as when a war ends—normal constitutional democracy would resume. But in a world where the war on terrorism has already persuaded us that we should favour security at all costs, even at the expense of incursions into public freedoms and private lives—in a world where every gesture, every word, every journey, every transaction can be monitored—these emergency measures could easily become permanent. Especially if there is a possibility that the virus might seasonally recur for several years.

The odds are that few among our fellow citizens will oppose them. One of the first lessons we have learnt in the current crisis is that authoritarian regimes, those governments that are controlling and paternalistic and impose strict social control, also seem the best equipped to deal with the dangers swiftly and effectively.

From that point of view, the less-than-appealing image projected by Western democracies during the pandemic is likely to have negative repercussions on democracy itself.

I realize that the viewpoints I have talked about are far from reassuring. But inasmuch as they represent plausible, or even probable developments, I cannot avoid mentioning them. A writer is a watchman; when the house in on fire, it is his responsibility to wake the residents, not leave them to sleep and wish them sweet dreams. Even so, I refuse to give in to despair, to disillusionment, to resignation. I am still convinced that a sea change is possible, and it seems to me that what has just happened will help us realize this, and take action.

Many of our contemporaries felt that the world was in a bad way before this crisis. But it was a vague, uncertain, nebulous impression, one that had no tangible form. Perhaps we were simply unaware of any imminent danger. Now we know that it is there. Omnipresent, ineradicable, disturbing. None of the passengers aboard the ship that is mankind can now ignore the fact that there are icebergs in our path, and that we must avoid them at all costs.

Paris, April, 2020

FRANK WYNNE is a literary translator and writer. Born in Ireland, he moved to France in 1984 where he discovered a passion for language. He began translating literature in the late 1990s, and in 2001 decided to devote himself to this full-time. He has translated works by Michel Houellebecq, Frédéric Beigbeder, Ahmadou Kourouma, Virginie Despentes, Tómas Eloy Martínez, and Javier Cercas. His work has earned him a number of awards, including the Scott Moncrieff Prize and the Premio Valle Inclán. Most recently, his translation of *Animalia* by Jean-Baptiste del Amo won the Republic of Consciousness Prize 2020.